D0489494

How to Change the World

The essential guide for social sector leaders

CRAIG DEARDEN-PHILLIPS

TURNPIKE PRESS

Cultivating Change

Turnpike Press
Wymondham
NR18 9SS
www.turnpikepress.co.uk

First published in Great Britain in 2017

ISBN 978-0-9559632-1-6

British Library Cataloguing-in-Publication Data
A catalogue record for this book is available from the British Library

Cover design by Carl Byrne
Illustrations by Jim Goreham
Typeset by Born London
Printed and bound in Great Britain by Clays
The publisher's policy is to use paper manufactured from
sustainable forests.

Introducing…Social Club

 Social Club is a unique place for a new generation of social sector leaders to come together, share, learn and have a voice. This book is one expression of that voice, with many of our profiled leaders here also members of the Club.

Social Club starts with the understanding that successful social change now and in the future relies on great leadership. This means helping today's social leaders to identify and fulfil their true potential. It also means helping people in very tough jobs to succeed in the rest of their lives, too.

To join Social Club, therefore, is a commitment not only to your professional development as a leader, but also to your own personal development. For, to be fit for the long-haul, you need to know yourself, be in balance and maintain a level of emotional control, even when all hell is breaking loose. At Social Club, we don't pretend leadership is easy. Indeed, we start from the premise that it's very easy to get it wrong: for your organisation as well as yourself.

Social Club membership offers the opportunity to meet with fellow leaders up to 10 times a year at our networking events held around the country. At these events, you hear from distinctive speakers from a variety of worlds, often beyond the social sector.

The Club is a place to grow, so we offer on top, bespoke one-to-one coaching, breakthrough events for senior teams, a peer-led advisory service and a range of smaller themed events throughout the year, where you can find solutions to the biggest issues facing you and your organisation.

Social Club is also about having a voice as a leader. We help leaders develop their voice individually and as a group through our social media channels, podcasts and publications. We help you as a social sector leader carry your influence further and faster both inside and beyond the organisation.

There are no formal entry bars to Social Club. Your organisation can be large or small, a charity, a CIC or private. Informally, we look for thoughtful leaders who want to get better, want to share and have more of a voice. If this is you, then get in touch and we can talk.

Craig Dearden-Phillips: http://SocialClubUK.com

I dedicate this book to my late mother,

Margaret Dearden

14 August 1944 – 26 January 2015

Contents

Foreword: Rt Hon. Norman Lamb MP

Introduction

Section 1: Transformation Leadership
Mark Atkinson, CEO, Scope
Julie Bentley, CEO, GirlGuiding
Chris Sherwood, CEO, Relate

Section 2: Entrepreneurial Leadership
Paul Sinton-Hewitt, Founder, Parkrun
Brett Wigdortz, Founder, Teach First
Sam Conniff, Co-founder and Chief Purpose
Officer, Livity

Section 3: Digital Leadership
Zoe Peden, Founder, Iris Speaks
Philip Colligan, CEO, RaspberryPiFoundation
Fiona Nielsen, CEO, Repositive

Section 4: Cultural Leadership
Lesley Dixon, CEO, PSS
Thomas Lawson, CEO, Leap Confronting
Conflict

Simon Blake, CEO, National Union of
Students

Section 5: Team Leadership
           Janet Tuohy, CEO, Aspire CIC
           Matt Hyde, CEO, The Scout Association
           Kuljit Sandhu, MD, RISE CIC

Section 6: Turnaround Leadership
           Kirsty McHugh, CEO, ERSA
           Rob Parkinson, CEO, Home-Start UK
           Matt Stevenson-Dodd, CEO, Street League

Section 7: Charismatic Leadership
           Sat Singh, CEO, Renaissance Foundation
           Dawn Hewitt, CEO, CHUMS CIC
           Kevin Davis, CEO, The Vine Trust

Section 8: Funder Leadership
           Nat Sloane, Chair, Big Lottery
           Andy Ratcliffe, CEO, Impetus-PEF
           Ben Rick, Managing Partner, SASC

Section 9: Future Leadership
           Karl Wilding, Director of Policy and
           Volunteering, NVCO
           Andy Hillier, Editor, Third Sector
           Professor Andy Wood, CEO, Adnams plc

Section 10: Your Leadership
           Reading list
           Index

Foreword by Norman Lamb MP

Changing the world isn't easy, whether you are a politician, as I am, or running a charity or social business.

Which is why this book is so welcome.

All of the social leaders featured here offer precious pointers to others who have dedicated their careers to making a direct difference in the world.

What I like about Craig's book is that nobody is pretending they have all the answers. Successfully changing the world is about more than running an organisation really well. It is also about building the right alliances, making compromises and accepting that change is a long-game, sometimes a lifetime's work.

Rather like in politics.

My own interest in social change has been informed by my

own family's direct experiences: our oldest son, diagnosed with Obsessive Compulsive Disorder at the age of 16 and my oldest sister who took her own life.

We have witnessed too many failures of the system. This has informed my own as a politician and a campaigner for better mental health services for all.

The very best social change organisations do not only show a better way to help people but they also influence the way a problem is perceived. Many of the organisations featured here do both. For that reason alone, this is a book that everyone should read.

If you lead in the social sector, or hold any ambition to do so, there is no better preparation than this excellent book.

'*It is very important to know who you are. To make decisions. To show who you are.*'

Malala Yousafzai

Author's Note

Writing a book is a labour of love. Everything else goes to one side, including the day job and family life, as you sit wondering how you're ever going to get it all done.

This book feels very special to me. I've learned a great deal while writing it. I've completed it feeling more committed than ever to leaders like you who choose to devote their career to changing the world.

I owe thanks to far too many people to name individually here. Particular thanks go to Robert Ashton, my publisher at Turnpike Press, who also conducted and drafted several of the interviews.

Thanks also to my colleague Jo Probitts at Stepping Out, to my long-term editor, Mark Griffiths, and to my coach Iain Hasdell for their personal support.

And, of course, to my partner, Katy, and our three kids, Ruby, Wilf and Arthur, who witness all my ups and downs.

I also want to thank all the contributing leaders who gave us such strong material for the book, not all of whom we have been able to include. I hope I have done this justice. Your generosity on all levels has made everything here possible.

Introduction

Everyone I have met who is a leader in the social sector starts out believing they can change the world. But they often find that making a clear, measurable difference isn't easy. Few, by mid-career, are achieving quite as much impact as they anticipated. Some leaders settle for that and focus on having a decent career.

Others don't sit back. Instead, they look to take their effectiveness as a social sector leader to another level. But where to go for help? One sees lots of 'Secrets of Success' books by business gurus and entrepreneurs about being a business success. Very little exists for the social sector that explores what makes for greater success. And vanishingly little brings the wisdom of our top social sector leaders to the fore. Hence this book, now.

Before I wrote this book, I asked myself some big questions:

Why this book – and why now?
One reason is personal. I bowed out of front-line leadership

before I was 40. I spent 14 years as CEO of a social sector organisation I founded when I was 25. I left exhausted, frustrated and feeling psychologically incapable of doing a similar job again.

My life had changed. Kids had arrived, money was suddenly tighter. I felt pressure on all sides. While a highly successful young leader by any conventional measures, it didn't actually feel that way inside. I was burnt out and left my CEO job not fully convinced I had done enough to justify the MBE I was offered.

So I forged a different life – helping current and future leaders across all sectors not only on how to make a bigger difference at the sharp end, but also to last the course, enjoy themselves and have a better balance.

The other reason I sat down to write this book is that after many conversations with many different social leaders, I believe I now have some powerful things to say about how leaders can really change the world for the better into the 2020s.

I have been helped massively in this by the people documented in this book. This has enabled a resource for leaders like you on how to be more successful. Not just in terms of visible achievement, but also inner success: how to remain strong, happy and balanced while also making a bigger impact in the world.

Who is this book for?
This is a book for social sector leaders, current and future. You might run a charity, a Community Interest Company or a co-operative. Alternatively, you may lead a spin-out

from the public sector or have a business that you run primarily for social purpose. Or you may be looking to lead one day. In short, if you are here to change the world, this book is for you.

It's important to say that this is not a book packed full of CEOs from the glamorous end of the social sector. There are some here, of course, but I felt it was important to include a range of interesting people to whom you, the reader, can relate.

To this end, I consciously strove to cast the net wide. You will therefore find leaders of very small organisations as well as the big charity brands. You'll see people from Leicester and Liverpool as well as London. And you will meet leaders from a range of social backgrounds, from middle-class Oxbridge to people who never finished school. Because this is our sector.

How the book is organised

How to curate a book like this, containing 27 personal profiles, presented a challenge. Leaders in our sector often defy easy categorisation. Nevertheless, for ease of navigation, I've organised the book into ten main sections:

Section 1: Transformational Leadership introduces a group of leaders who have taken large organisations on a long-term journey of radical change, based on a new understanding of the world they are operating in and its needs.

Section 2: Entrepreneurial Leadership highlights the role that three entrepreneurial leaders have played to grow the social mission of their organisations. Interestingly this includes setting up privately owned social ventures.

Section 3: Digital Leadership focuses on the powerful ways in which a group of forward-thinking social sector leaders are harnessing the power of digital technology to take social impact to whole new levels, often without the need for an equivalent growth in resources.

Section 4: Cultural Leadership groups people who have, in a variety of ways, challenged and changed the values, beliefs and behaviours of an organisation they have led, enabling their organisations to raise their social impact.

Section 5: Team Leadership looks at the challenges for social sector leaders of building top quality teams who are capable of taking impact to the next level.

Section 6: Turnaround Leadership brings together a group of leaders who have all led a rapid improvement in their organisations' short-term fortunes, keeping the lights on and enabling them to successfully plan for the longer term.

Section 7: Charismatic Leadership looks at the particular upsides and downsides of this approach to leadership in social sector organisations.

Section 8: Funder Leadership gives us insight into the way progressive social sector leaders in the fields of grant-making and social finance are responding to a challenging financial environment.

Section 9: Future Leadership asks what those who study key trends in our sector see as the key leadership challenges of the 2020s.

Section 10: Your Leadership is a 'workshop' chapter designed to help you to locate where you are now on your personal leadership journey, the difference you seek to make going forward and how you're doing to do this.

What's your End-Game?

Social sector leadership is about making the biggest possible impact on the totality of the problem you seek to address. As you'll see, this isn't necessarily about creating a big organisation. In truth, few social sector organisations achieve the break-through scale needed to solve an entire problem. Changing the world is just as often achieved by having your ideas and work carried forward by others, including governments. A big part of social sector leadership is knowing your 'end-game' – figuring just how your organisation can maximise its influence on problems you exist to solve.

Top ten tips

So, what are the 'Top Ten Tips' from my book for social sector leaders seeking a bigger impact?

1. **Lead from behind**. The most successful social sector leaders lead from behind as much as from the front. They lead organisations that people join by choice as much as financial necessity, be they staff or volunteers. So, outside of turnaround situations, leadership is more about engagement – convenor of the organisation rather than its commander.

Key behaviours: Talk to more people, in more depth. Listen more than you talk.

2. **Build coalitions.** If they want to make things happen, leaders in the social sector have to build coalitions both

inside and beyond the organisation. The authority invested in leadership in this sector is probably less than in the private sector, where the CEO is given more latitude. To get people on board, CEOs leading big transformation need to develop strong political skills.

Key behaviours: Plan who you need to deliver change. Think about what aspects will get each group on board.

3. **Be authentic.** The most successful leaders are genuine people who stay human. It sounds simple, but we all know that the pressures in organisations often mean that leaders sometimes fail in this regard. Authenticity in social sector leadership isn't the same thing as being liked. It's about people knowing that you are authentic, stand for particular values and that you uphold them, come what may.

Key behaviours: Make clear what you believe. Prove this through your behaviour.

4. **Be ambitious.** Leaders who are really changing the world are those with a vast ambition around the mission and how it can be grown. They create a sense of possibility beyond what is currently being achieved. Their skill is doing this without demeaning past achievement. And framing the future in a way that pays back to staff, volunteers and others, the organisation's sense of its true purpose.

Key behaviours: Think big, encourage others to do the same. Frame ambition squarely in the language of mission.

5. **Think impact.** First-order social sector leaders are making their organisations think hard about how to capture

and communicate the difference they make (or not!). For many organisations - habituated to reporting activity not results - this is difficult. But, if the world is to be changed, those leading it have to be clear on progress. The first step is tactfully making the challenge about the difference the organisation is making, in a way that people can cope with.

Key behaviours: Cold honesty, openness, comfort with laying down a challenge.

6. **Create your culture**. Top social sector leaders understand that, for an organisation to make an impact, it has to have the right culture. When coming in new, social leaders often find a culture that's getting in the way of progress. 'Show me the Leader, Show me the Culture' is a cliché, but one with some truth. While aspects of culture can remain immune to a leader's influence, the best leaders waste no time setting out the attitudes and behaviour that they most value.

Key behaviours: Make people aware of your values and expectations of everyone. Repeat it often and model it yourself.

7. **Get your team right**. Successful social sector leaders put great store by a top team which is capable, even when this means tough choices. They understand that this unit is the key to success or failure, the A Team. And that a B Team won't change the world. Therefore, finding a top team where people trust and challenge each other, sharing in success or failure together, is essential to success.

Key behaviours: Set a high bar on senior colleagues. Look for alignment or core values, but also a diverse range of perspectives.

8. **Coach, don't manage.** The very best social sector leaders tend to act like coaches rather than bosses. In relation to the people around them, they see their primary task as drawing out the best. They know that micro-managing is a waste of time. They understand that needing to manage someone closely is a sure sign of a bigger problem. They also use their coaching skills to help people see when it's time to go or take on a new role.

Key behaviours: Think of yourself as an enabler, not a manager. Allow people to manage their own detail.

9. **Be visible.** The best social sector leaders are rarely found in their office. They understand that their key role is to be engaging with people both inside and beyond the organisation. Visibility is the hallmark of the successful, effective social sector CEO. This isn't about 'turning up' to set-piece events, like a visiting dignitary. It's about making yourself available to people to talk to, be questioned by. Or, if needs be, take criticism from.

Key behaviours: Get out of your 'bubble'. Move around the organisation, putting yourself 'on the line', even if uncomfortable.

10. **Look after yourself.** The most successful social sector leaders work hard, but they understand this is a long game. So, they tend to look after themselves. On a simple level, this is about time-out, the right diet, sleep and exercise. But, it's also about professional development: creating a good network of peers, working with a coach, subjecting yourself to new learning. Such is the demand on the personality of a social sector leader, that good self-care is critical.

Key behaviours: Better 'work-hygiene', developing support beyond the organisation.

In short, to change the world as a social sector leader, you have to make the most of the organisation you lead.

Good luck and happy reading!

SECTION ONE

TRANSFORMATIONAL LEADERSHIP

*'Turnover is Vanity,
Impact is Sanity.'*

**Neil Woodbridge, CEO,
Thurrock Lifestyle Solutions CIC**

Introduction

For as long as I can remember, there has been much talk in the social sector of transformation. It started in the crash in 2007, carried on through the Coalition and austerity, well beyond 2015.

Yet, evidence of doing things differently has been hard to come by. Faced with big choices about how to face the future, some social sector organisations turn the other way, afraid perhaps, of unpalatable choices.

The trope is familiar: spend the reserves, hope things will get better, make small changes around the edges (talking these up as you go). But, the overall idea of how your organisation operates is not challenged. It stays the same, only smaller. Nothing is fundamentally rethought about how the organisation creates the difference it is here to make.

Sound at all familiar?

Transformational leadership involves a fundamental rethink about how an organisation can make the biggest difference. This requires not only imagination and political skills, but also a steady nerve.

3

Transformational leaders are willing to rock the boat, at least initially, by laying down three big challenges to everyone around them:

'What's our 'End Game' - what are we here to do?'
'How is the world around us changing?'
'How different do we need to look to make an impact on that world?'

business model

In making such challenges, transformational leaders open themselves to risks that wouldn't otherwise surface. As you may have found yourself, asking the big questions doesn't always go down well. Neither does criticism of how things are working now – even when it's plain to see they are not.

And, equally, an exciting new vision can easily be brought low by reasonable-sounding questions about its feasibility. Lacking the skills, energy or gumption to engage with the doubters, some social sector leaders choose the quiet life: competently managing decline rather than leading necessary change. Surviving but seldom thriving.

Hence this chapter. In here, I'm trying to showcase for you a number of leaders who, in very different ways, are being transformational.

We open with **Mark Atkinson** of Scope, who is attempting what may be the most ambitious transformation ever of a big-brand UK charity. Mark is turning Scope from a large scale provider of contracted services for disabled people into a smaller, digitally-enabled organisation, focusing on innovative new services and a stronger campaigning voice.

4

Julie Bentley is CEO of Girlguiding and has successfully taken on, among others, the *Daily Mail*, to reposition her organisation as part of the movement for female equality. Here we explore the journey she has taken Girlguiding on in recent years.

Chris Sherwood is the CEO of the charity Relate. Since his appointment at the tender age of 34, Chris has taken on the task of creating an online offer from Relate in addition to traditional channels. To do this, he is creating a much stronger national centre for Relate within an organisation that has been a federation since its foundation in the 1930s.

Mark Atkinson, CEO, Scope www.scope.org.uk @MarkAtScope

'You get one chance at this kind of transformation. What's really going to kill or cure the organisation is getting the future offer right, maintaining the Scope brand equity while moving out of one set of activities and into another.'

Operation enormous

Mark Atkinson had been in his job of Director of External Affairs at national disability charity Scope for just 19 months when the opportunity arose to lead the organisation on an interim basis.

Although it was the first such opportunity Mark had been offered, he accepted and his appointment as CEO was made permanent six months later. A couple of years on, Mark is leading what is arguably the biggest single transformation of a large charity that the UK has seen.

SCOPE
- *Scope* is a charity whose mission is to ensure disabled people have the same opportunities as everyone else
- Formed as The Spastics' Society in 1952, the organisation changed its name to Scope in 1994 to better reflect its positive approach to opportunities for disabled people
- When Mark Atkinson took up the position of CEO in 2015, he embarked the charity upon the most ambitious single transformation of a large national charity ever attempted.

Young, open and generous

When you meet Mark, a couple of things immediately strike you. The first is his relative youth. In his late 30s, Mark is one of our youngest senior leaders. The second is his openness. Mark is keen to share the radical change he is trying, with his Board, to create. The fact that Scope's change-journey has some risks makes Mark's generosity all the more impressive. And, if you are looking to learn, massively helpful.

But first, who is Mark Atkinson? Born in Lancaster in the late 1970s, he grew up in an ordinary family, worked hard at school and went on to do A levels at a college in Somerset, where his father was then living. After completing his studies, he spent a year as President of the Students' Union. Successful at this, he stood for election as a National Vice President of the National Union of Students. This pitched the young Mark into London and all sorts of interesting work in policy and politics.

Working for the big break

After all that, Mark found transitioning into a 'proper' job quite hard. His first was working in the press office of the Local Government Association (LGA). He spent two happy years there before being sent to Brussels to help the LGA think about how councils could get early-warning on new EU initiatives. *'This was a policy job and required me to be more proactive and take a longer term view – I developed different – but complimentary – skills from those I had gained working in a busy and news driven press office.'*

After almost a decade of policy and communications jobs with Citizens Advice, the Youth Sport Trust and Ambitious about Autism, Mark got his big break at Scope as Director of External Affairs at Scope before he was asked to act as Interim CEO just 13 months in.

Scoping Scope

To Mark's newcomer eyes, Scope was highly preoccupied with its large contracted service delivery businesses. This degree of absorption, he felt, *'made it harder for Scope to have a really sharp campaigning message and, perhaps more importantly, to respond imaginatively to the needs of disabled people in the 2020s.'*

Once confirmed as CEO six months later, Mark started testing his thinking. He commissioned extensive research on the needs and views of disabled people and their families both within and beyond Scope. He also looked systematically at where the gaps were in current provision and issues where the influence of disabled people could be improved.

The result of this work was sobering: the vast majority of Scope's resources were aimed at running contracted services for a few thousand people. The quality of these services was very good with the portfolio sitting considerably above the national average.

However, the portfolio (which included residential care homes, supported living services, a fostering agency, schools, a college, and a children home) was losing significant money. They had never been run to make a profit but in fact were making a considerable loss as a result of rising costs and downward pressure on statutory income. The future offer to disabled people was, in Mark's words, *'somewhere between non-existent and incoherent.'*

Ways to go
Mark and his Board now faced a three-way fork in the road: slowly evolve Scope's services and overall offer to a better place; merge with a similar charity; or do something completely different.

The first two options didn't feel right to Mark and most of his Board. Scope's services, while pioneering in their day, were now the industry standard. Running them as Scope-branded services no longer felt imperative. A merger, while possible, felt like an opportunity lost. The alternative was to go back to Scope's founding principles and values and create, a fresh, pioneering, innovative and influential organisation. And this is what won the day.

Making it happen
None of this, Mark underlines, is easy. There are three major leadership challenges, he explains – *'all of which could fill a CEO's week.'*

The first is to find exceptional providers for the bulk of Scope's remaining care and education services, 40% of Scope's current turnover.

The second is to rapidly develop a brand-new set of offers for disabled people, many of them online.

The third is to build up Scope again as an organisation of voice and influence spanning all disabled people.

To get an idea of the sheer scale of change here, the turnover of Scope will initially go down from about £90m in 2017 to £50m by 2020. However, Mark is firmly of the view that this transformative restructure will in fact enable Scope to grow back to its current turnover within the next seven to 10 years. In the meantime, the number of direct employees will drop from nearly 3,000 to less than 1,000.

Risks and fears

I ask Mark about the risks and how he feels about them. He is clear in his response. *'The risks of doing nothing are much higher.'* He is keen to avoid the trap he thinks many charities fall into of talking transformation while walking a much more conservative line.

Mark realises he could have an easier life doing things in an evolutionary way, but that is simply not his approach. If anything keeps him up at night – as well as his two small children – it is a realisation that he probably has one opportunity to get this right.

I put it to Mark that many readers will want to attempt transformational change but don't know how. There is no single approach, Mark says, but the first thing is to ask the big questions. In his case, *'What will be the relevance of Scope to the lives of disabled people in 21st century Britain? This is the cornerstone. From here, you get to questions of strategy, offer and, finally, the future shape and size of organisation.'*

Aligning management

But whatever the change, Mark is very clear that alignment with the Board is critical. *'The Board of Scope, like all Boards, has been on a long journey taking nearly two years to research, debate and consult on our new direction. Taking that time has been necessary. Now we need to make sure that implementation goes at a good pace.'*

During this period, Mark made several changes in his senior team with only one person remaining from when he became CEO. *'This was mainly about re-purposing the organisation – but also about getting people around you who are aligned with what you are trying to do.'*

How does someone leading a transformational change keep on top? This is a work-in-progress, Mark confesses. It was fed back on a 360-degree appraisal that he tends to model over-work.

'I take this stuff very seriously and feel personally accountable,' he explains, *'but I need to let go and feel more trusting. I need to get better at supporting others to take that space. I do take setbacks personally. I have to work hard at my personal resilience. I have incredibly hard standards and can be unforgiving on myself and others around me.'*

Key Points from Mark:

1. Transformation is something relatively few larger organisations appear to be doing – managing decline is often the reality.
2. Scope is seeking to restart the organisation from founding principles, asking what it needs to do to be more relevant to disabled people's lives today.
3. Transitioning from a £90m service delivery organisation to a smaller one with a new service offer means that Scope's current services will need to move to new providers.
4. Social leadership in this context means being courageous enough to ask the big existential questions.
5. A major new strategy needs a generous amount of time to develop but once decided needs to be implemented with pace.

Julie Bentley, CEO, Girlguiding
www.girlguiding.org.uk @juliebentley

'The key to being effective is being really clear about what you're offering, what you expect – and being consistent and authentic. I set that clear expectation.'

Life beyond the police
Julie Bentley, CEO of Girlguiding, doesn't come across as the squeamish sort. But she is. And, in many ways, it's a good job. At 18, Julie was working for the police as a trainee photographic technician, processing explicit crime photographs from across Essex, a job she knew, pretty much from day one, wasn't for her.

Ignoring her boss's pleas, Julie left the police and worked for Royal Mail as a postwoman for five years. At the same time, she volunteered as a youth worker to gain experience and training. In her early 20s, she got her first youth work job – in London, with the Charterhouse charity in Southwark.

That certain something

Julie remembers the interview with Beth, her first CEO, extremely well. Julie wasn't the most experienced or best qualified person that day. But Beth saw something in her. Indeed, that person could see that Julie would go all the way and she remains a good friend. This has informed the type of CEO Julie has become as leader of the biggest and fastest-growing voluntary association for girls and young women in Britain.

Julie Bentley comes across as a clear, unencumbered communicator. She doesn't relate things in the abstract or resort to the studied language quite common in our sector. Leaving school at 18, finding work and only later gaining her MBA through the Open University, Julie has learned to rub along well with all sorts of people.

It sounds strange to say, but you very quickly know where you are with Julie – this is one of her signature strengths. She combines a direct approach with the empathy you'd expect in someone who has spent a lifetime in youth work. But there's an element of 'don't mess' too, which you hope to find in any top CEO.

GIRLGUIDING
- Girlguiding is the charity behind Rainbows, Brownies, Guides and Rangers
- A membership organisation consisting of over 100,000 volunteers, 27,000 groups meeting every week, half a million members and a waiting list of 77,000 girls
- Appointed Chief Executive of Girlguiding in 2012, Julie Bentley set about a complete governance review, developing the organisation's first five year strategy and changing its Promise, so that members commit to 'develop my beliefs' rather than 'love my God'.

An enthusiasm for mergers

Girlguiding is Julie's fourth CEO job. She cut her teeth at a small charity working with people with alcohol issues – a baptism of fire as the organisation was about to go under. This led to her taking the charity into a merger after six months, which has left her with an enthusiasm for mergers that continues today.

Following a directorship in the merged organisation, Julie became CEO of the Suzy Lamplugh Trust five years later, working closely with the Founder, Paul, who was father of the estate agent who disappeared in the mid-1980s. This was a tough job, requiring both sensitivity and firmness. Julie's next step was to become CEO of the Family Planning Association.

Then came Girlguiding, a choice Julie made through her passion for women's issues, young people and the excitement of leading a large female focussed organisation.

Transforming the organisations

When Julie arrived, her in-tray was pretty full. Three major issues loomed. The first was an outdated public perception of the charity and the need for it to proudly shift its place in the public consciousness. Julie felt that a break with the past was needed – that Girlguiding needed to be about future women and their place in the world. The second was the need to overhaul the charity's cumbersome and outdated governance structures. The third was the challenge posed by a very different compliance culture than was the case just 20 years ago. Children are thankfully much better protected than they were – but this has meant massive changes in the way that voluntary bodies like Girlguiding operate.

An overarching challenge was fundraising. Historically, Girlguiding relied mainly on subscriptions. If anything, it raised money to give away to other deserving causes. Today, Girlguiding raises £2m a year from a mix of sources, including strategically aligned corporate partners – the likes of Rolls-Royce who want, quite rightly, to encourage young women to think about their sector as one in which they can have a future.

Transforming the culture

Julie is very clear that leadership is about setting a culture - about being visible and being open to people. She has worked hard to establish a personal reputation of authenticity and visibility.

To this end, she is active on Twitter and communicates directly with volunteers, staff and the wider charity sector. She also gets out and about, both at Girlguiding events but also sector-wide events.

This wasn't the culture on Julie's arrival in 2015. At first, when she spoke to people in the kitchen and elsewhere, they looked at her oddly, unused to being addressed directly by the CEO. Indeed, they were suspicious – *'top managers traditionally sent a PA down to get their coffee.'*

Having minions, however, isn't Julie's style. *'Being accessible means being normal and open,'* she says. Julie does staff inductions herself and personally facilitates the weekly staff consultation group with reps from across the staff team. *'People need to know who I am if they are to trust me as their CEO,'* she tells me. Julie uses a lot of humour to make people relax but also makes clear she has high expectations and will hold people to account.

Transforming the organisation
Julie's open style isn't born of a need to be popular. Since her appointment, she has challenged Girlguiding hard on a number of fronts. She has made big changes to head office, reducing headcount and overseeing the lease of half of the former head office to a hotel group. She has introduced hot-desking and got rid of her own private office, preferring to sit in an open area.

Following the development of the charity's first five-year strategic plan, Julie instigated a thoroughgoing restructure, to align the HQ team around the delivery of the strategy. This led to a several redundancies of long standing senior staff and the creation of a number of new roles that better met the needs of the organisation.

Today only 20% of staff in head office were there when Julie started in 2015. *'You can't,'* she says, *'go into an organisation that needs change and be popular with everyone. You have to accept that. You have to push hard, trust yourself that you are operating with the best intentions – and that way people trust you.'*

More collaboration, less holding on
Julie looks at the future of the sector and sees the need for deeper and wider collaboration. She believes that this will save resources and improve what is on offer. The youth sector is, she thinks, in the vanguard of change here. Many of the top organisations' CEOs want to further collaborate, she tells me. *'CEOs in the youth sector like and trust each other and want to take whatever co-operation means to the next level.'*

However, Julie recognises that the wider social sector has a way to go. *'We all have to think about what is best for the organisation,'* she notes. *'A lot of organisations see their beneficiaries as 'theirs'. They won't always think about what is best for the beneficiary, if that means they lose the funding associated with that same person.'*

A fine line on talent
The other thing Julie is passionate about is future talent. As someone who was 'spotted' and given huge encouragement in her early career, she has a fervour for finding and developing the next generation of leaders.

Here, Julie has to watch herself a little. She recognises a fine line between the perception of her as a developer of people and a sponsor of the favoured. But, despite this, Julie has active conversations with her people at key points in their careers about where they are going. And often, these are about telling people that they might not be cut out for CEO and to find their success in another direction.

Road to resilience

For Julie, life as a CEO is frequently chaotic and unclear. *'You have to learn to live with that.'* You also have to avoid striving for perfection, as this doesn't enable you to get enough done.

Big on talking things through, Julie often seeks colleagues' advice both inside and beyond the organisation. She has become better at observing boundaries. Julie stays away from work emails in the evenings and during those weekends she has free. WhatsApp works really well, she tells me, for emergency communications, negating the need for constant checking of email. This has helped to build her resilience.

The overwhelming message from Julie is that how you go about the role matters as much as the decisions you make as CEO.

'When you walk into the office, you set the tone for that day. That is the power you have as CEO, whether you like it or not.'

Julie knows that the small things matter. It is for this reason that she writes personally to staff who are leaving to thank them for their contribution, as well as welcoming all new staff with a handwritten card. This, she says, is the way to achieve influence up and down a large organisation: *'People need to know who you are and that they matter to you as their leader.'*

In just a few years, Julie has led the transformation of Girlguiding both internally and in the public mind. This has meant being willing, when necessary, to face down the doubters, including the *Daily Mail*, who questioned whether Girlguiding should be seen as part of the feminist movement. At the time of writing, this already feels like ancient history; evidence that at least one aspect of Girlguiding's transformation to have been a resounding success.

Key Points from Julie:
1. The hands-on experience of leading a small charity can be good preparation for taking on a bigger transformation challenge.
2. Twitter and 'turning up' can make it easier for your front-line staff to connect with you and feel you understand.
3. Overhead costs can grow slowly. Only when viewed through fresh eyes can assumptions be challenged and premises and staff roles reviewed.
4. Collaboration is going to be key – are there organisations with which you could share costs and resources with – or more?
5. Chaos is to be expected. Your team can handle the routines leaving you to deal with the unexpected.

Chris Sherwood, CEO, Relate
www.relate.org.uk @RelateChris

'As our services increasingly move online, where you physically are becomes less important than what you deliver.'

A 21st century approach
To appoint a 34-year-old openly gay man as Chief Executive of Relate shows just how far the organisation has gone to shake off its blue rinse reputation.

Formerly the Marriage Guidance Council (until 1988), Relate had been led by almost exclusively by married women of a certain age. Since his appointment in 2015, Chris's main effort has been to shape the Relate organisation and offer to the way people live today: online, on their phone, in a market full of choices.

RELATE
- Relate was founded in 1938 as the National Marriage Guidance Council, by a clergyman who was concerned about the impact of modern life on marriage
- After the Second World War, Relate grew very quickly, helping people through the almost inevitable relationship turbulence that follows a major social upheaval like war
- CEO since 2015, Chris Sherwood is now leading the digital transformation of this household name.

Steel and trouble

Like many social sector leaders, Chris's early life was not straightforward. He was born in the early 1980s into a working-class family in Corby in the East Midlands. The town's steel industry was in precipitant decline, leaving poverty and lack of opportunity in its wake.

Sadly, Chris experienced troubled relationships with his mother and father, both of whom were dependent on alcohol. Nevertheless, Chris was bright and resilient. He excelled at school and, although he wasn't sure of his future path, he could see Higher Education as his way out. He duly became the first member of his family not only to finish school with five good GCSEs, but even to attend university.

Chris left Corby for Exeter University to study History and Society. But, in the absence of the 'Bank of Mum and Dad', he needed to support himself through college. So, at the age of 19 he worked for Plymouth City Council as a junior bid writer. Here he acquired a mentor, Bill Hande, who was then a Director at Devon County Council. Bill was the first person to 'spot' Chris and his talent. He inspired Chris to take on a comparable role for other young people making their way.

Work took Chris to London in his 20s where he performed a range of operational and business development roles for NESTA, the Shaw Trust and Scope before joining Relate to head up policy and communications.

Surprise choice

Chris's appointment as CEO of Relate took some in the sector by surprise, not least because it was his first ever CEO role. His pitch for the job involved sharing his own regret that he had not used the charity's services ahead of his own relationship breakdown with his civil partner a few years earlier. Part of Chris's offer to the organisation was to make Relate more accessible to people like him: younger, not in traditional set-ups and faced with lots of choice as to where to get support – some far more customer-friendly than that of Relate!

While delighted to get the CEO job, being in Relate already gave him a *'shorter honeymoon period, as people expected me to know stuff already and not ask so many questions.'*

Shifting mission

'Poor quality relationships are often at the root of so many problems,' Chris tells me, *'including poor mental health, homelessness, debt and loneliness.'* And Relate's mission remains to provide effective relationship support to everyone who needs it, no matter what their circumstances or relationship background.

But, while the charity adapted well to the growing diversity of relationships, it was struggling with the way people want to receive relationship support.

Chris explains: '*To get a service from Relate was, until recently, actually quite hard, with clients waiting far longer than they would like.*' He contrasts this with the instant online couples counselling now available via smartphones, linked to the booming therapy market to those in need of services. No forms, no phone numbers, no fuss.

From in line to online
So, a big transformation challenge for Chris has been bringing Relate's offer into line with the market and building a coalition in favour of change among key groups involved in delivering Relate's services.

This includes relationship counsellors, Relate's permanent staff and the various Relate organisations in the federation. The degree of change required has needed a big investment in new resources, including digital technology.

Digital technology features large in Chris Sherwood's work as a thought-leader in the social sector. It is, he notes, the cause of much relationship strife, and increasingly, the way people today seek help.

'*Digital infidelity, online porn and using the internet to hook up with former partners, can disrupt a relationship,*' Chris says. '*Yet the ability to provide counselling and information online – via webcam, instant chat and email – also makes it far easier for couples with problems to access support. It's the perfect accompaniment to our face-to-face services.*'

The Relate website now offers the opportunity for 'live chat' with an experienced counsellor. *'It makes sense to use the technology that led to a relationship breakdown as you try to mend it.'*

Moving at pace

As with any federated charity, relationships can be tense between individual Relate organisations and the national body. Not everyone handles change well, yet you can't move at the pace of the slowest in the team.

And with less public investment in third sector capacity, the ability to grow earned income is important to Relate. Indeed, you don't have to go far into the Relate website to find yourself facing a PayPal pay-wall.

But on this Chris is clear: *'Whilst we will always be there for those who cannot pay for our services, our paid offer is going to keep growing for busy people looking for help here and now.'*

Leader of leaders

Chris describes his leadership style as open, accessible and transparent. As a leader, he says your authenticity cannot be a mask; you have to be real; you have to be you. He's actually found that the change from senior manager to CEO has required him to bring more of his personal life into work.

'Leading a charity is never going to be a nine to five job, and people need to know you as a person, as well as a leader if they are to follow. And, as each Relate centre is an independent charity, each with its own CEO and Chair, I am really a leader of leaders.'

In common with many social leaders featured in this book, Chris also describes the sense of loneliness you can feel when the boss. He has a great Board, but also maintains a strong network of trusted peers.

Not surprisingly, the CEO of Relate believes in sharing problems before they become overwhelming.

Key Points from Chris:
1. **The learning curve can be gentler if you already work for the organisation you go on to lead. Equally, there is a danger you will assume more and challenge less.**
2. **Technology is a double-edged sword that every organisation has to learn to handle.**
3. **Growing your earned income gives you choice over the direction your organisation takes.**
4. **You have to be passionate about the change your organisation is striving to achieve. Any lack of authenticity will quickly be spotted.**
5. **Change in a federation involves coalition building skills as a leader.**

SECTION TWO

ENTREPRENEURIAL LEADERSHIP

'No-one is going to tell you what to do when you are MD of a start-up business like this. The Board are there to help, but if you want to see change, you have to lead it yourself.'

Kat Sowden, Managing Director, Persona Care and Support Ltd

Introduction

Entrepreneurial Leadership is about fashioning a new business out of new or borrowed ideas. As it's how I started my own leadership journey as a 25-year-old, this type of leadership has always been interesting for me.

What is entrepreneurial leadership? It's marked out by some clear traits. One is creativity. All entrepreneurs, social or otherwise, have a drive to create new things from scratch. In the social sector, the added factor is that leaders want to create new things for which there is social benefit above and beyond just meeting a direct customer need.

The term 'social entrepreneur' is often used to describe people like **Paul Sinton-Hewitt**, founder of Parkrun and **Brett Wigdortz**, founding CEO of Teach First and **Sam Conniff** of Livity, who all feature here. As you will see, success for them is measured primarily by their social impact, not by how successfully their venture enriches its founders and investors.

The second marker of entrepreneurial leadership is drive. Having ideas is one thing. Two-a-penny, in fact. Executing them is something else altogether. The ability to attract early resources to an idea and create something of value requires both massive personal drive and the fortitude to survive setbacks. The three people featured here have experienced and survived this. It comes with the territory.

A later trait of successful entrepreneurial leaders is knowing the right time to pass on the baton. While all of these leaders have served long-spells as CEO, each has called time on themselves and brought in a new CEO. Then either taken, like Paul, a supporting role on the Board – or, like Brett and Sam, stepped right out.

Why is this so? There seems to be recognition in entrepreneurial leaders that the leadership skills required for starting a new venture and shepherding it through its initial growth are not necessarily those required for long-term stewardship. By and large, entrepreneurs tend not to enjoy management or the lead times to get things done once the organisation is bigger.

If you're new to the notion of social enterprise, you might ask whether it's possible to run a profitable social business and achieve social outcomes at the same time. Isn't there some kind of seesaw-like trade-off between a brilliant business and a social purpose? The answer is that, in a good social business, commercial and social success feed off each other. It's not 'either-or'.

Companies like Livity – co-founded by Sam Conniff – are social businesses whose business model requires commercial success to deliver social impact. The two are delivered at the same time, via the same process, not as distinct activities.

One thing marks out the entrepreneurial leader in the social sector from their brethren in the purely commercial world: reward. None of the people here has created anything like the personal wealth for themselves that would be possible in other sectors. While commercial success and social impact do go together, its proceeds flow overwhelmingly back into the organisation.

Whatever form it takes, Entrepreneurial Leadership requires guts, patience and a belief in what you're doing. And, it appears, awareness of when it's time to hand over to others.

Paul Sinton-Hewitt – Founder of parkrun
www.parkrun.org.uk @paulsintonhewit

'We are not trying to build the Microsoft or Google of running. We are simply helping communities to deliver these events in a professional and brilliant way.'

Go running

If, like me, you go running, you'll probably have done at least one parkrun. And if you don't, you will know someone who has. Because parkrun is now worldwide. Every Saturday morning, people in over 1,100 locations in 15 countries across the planet pull on their trainers and head to their local park – to make the start-line by 9.00am sharp with up to 1,000 fellow parkrunners.

One truly remarkable thing about parkrun is that every event – from Aberdeen to Adelaide – is *exactly* the same. 5km in length. Free of charge. Open to all. Run entirely by local volunteers.

While parkrun is a professionally timed event (you can look up your time online by lunchtime), there is no 'winner'. The only thing that is celebrated is participation. Nor is parkrun 'governed' as most running events are – you can push a pram, run with your dog or even cartwheel round if you wish! Commercial sponsorship is barely visible and the focus is on community.

PARKRUN
- parkrun is a limited company that organises free, weekly, 5km timed runs open to everyone, safe and easy to take part in
- The company is able to offer hundreds of free events across the country and around the world every week thanks largely to the fantastic support it receives from its partners
- parkrun began as an idea in the head of an injured middle-aged runner called Paul Sinton-Hewitt in 2004.

Small beginnings

Paul Sinton-Hewitt was part of his local running club, but wanted to create something *'open, free, really well run, in which anyone could take part, going at your own pace, no celebration of winning, being the best you can be.'*

The first parkrun event took place in Bushy Park, south-west London in 2004, attracting a scattering of people. Soon, a second event was taking place in another part of London. Then, a third and fourth.

It was clear to Paul, almost from the beginning, that parkrun had the potential to become what it is today. *'I never worried about growth, because the numbers were doubling every year right from the start.'* The challenge, for Paul, was to do this in a way that did not compromise the founding values: free, open to all and, most important, a community event led by volunteers.

The very early years of parkrun were not all-consuming for Paul. *'I wasn't under pressure to begin with. People approached me. I asked them searching questions to find what motivated them.'* And if they passed muster, they'd be given the rules and resources of parkrun free of charge. There was one condition: that they followed the 'rules' of parkrun – everything must be done in a set way on the ground to ensure that the ethos of parkrun is upheld.

Sticking to principles – no sell out
As parkrun grew, so did the pressures. By 2008, parkrun was employing staff and attracting the attention of potential big-money sponsors.

Although parkrun needed bigger investment to stay afloat, Paul sensed danger. He had learned, quite early on, that the big companies wouldn't just back parkrun for its own sake. *'I had to learn the hard way, that it's not how sponsorship works. Companies wanted things from me I wasn't prepared to give. They wanted sales – and I didn't allow them to sell.'*

So, huge offers from big global brands were politely declined. *'Coca Cola opened their chequebook – we didn't take it.'* And parkrun continued to live hand-to-mouth with backing from a small group of aligned sponsors who liked the organisation and were prepared to live with Paul's low-key approach.

Growing strains

The explosion in the popularity of parkrun after 2010 saw Paul's role as CEO evolve very quickly. Although the team at parkrun has always been relatively small, Paul had to adjust his approach. *'When I started, I did what I wanted, the things that made sense to me. I had a sense of moral purpose and was guided by that. As people came on board, I had to become more consultative. And the time came when I had to appoint a Chief Officer for the UK.'*

This was a difficult time for Paul. *'Now I had to start compromising, being consultative, having a Board in place.'* All of this was made harder by the sheer pace of growth and a tendency to clash at times with the person he had appointed to run parkrun UK (now happily resolved).

Succession

By 2014, after a decade at the helm, Paul hit a point of unhappiness in his role as overall CEO of parkrun.

'I was burning out, in the quagmire, at loggerheads, trying to be all things to all people and couldn't see what I needed to see.'

Paul realised it was time for him to give up the day-to-day leadership and take another role. He knew that, for parkrun to progress to its potential, it needed a fresh approach, someone who could develop a revised strategy, improve the organisation and attract the necessary resources.

In Paul's eyes, the arrival of Nick Pearson as the new global CEO saw many welcome changes. Nick had been CEO of Sweatshop, a sports retailer – and an 800m champion in his day. Shortly after Mike Ashley's Sports Direct bought

Sweatshop, Nick left and turned down several highly-paid jobs to lead parkrun. A natural collaborator, Nick quickly got the organisation into better shape, engineered a new strategy and attracted new sponsorship.

A new life

Today, in his mid-50s, Paul is a non-executive director and ambassador for parkrun, *'the happiest I have ever been.'* Asked about the future, he sounds disinclined to do it all again, as many founders do: *'I was a reluctant entrepreneur and I never set out to be a CEO, I didn't set out to do those things.'*

No longer full-time, Paul finds himself busy still with parkrun business, *'trying to get local governments and Athletic Associations across the world to see parkrun as an asset, not a threat.'* And, as a Board member, he continues to play a supporting rather than leading role.

Paul also spends time mentoring emerging people and is a Fellow of Ashoka, the global network of social entrepreneurs. He speaks regularly, though gets bored telling his story, *'a reluctant public speaker'*, preferring the interaction offered by Q&A.

Leadership lessons

In Paul's words, *'If you are using your values as your rudder, you are going to make decisions in light of this.'* When times were tough, parkrun could so easily have chosen to become the 'Coca Cola parkrun' – with Paul never having to fret about money again. But, to him, this would have ruined parkrun: *'The best thing anyone can do is to be clear about what they stand for, their values and beliefs and how these relate to what they are trying to do – or risk being led down a path.'*

Secondly, there is clearly a time in any founder's journey when one hits a point where the organisation's success depends on you passing the torch. Having the wisdom to see this and act on it is a powerful form of leadership. To continue, beyond this point – as many founders do – at best limits future success. At worst, it endangers the whole organisation.

The third leadership lesson from Paul and parkrun is less obvious but equally powerful – that, to make a huge impact, you do not need to become a giant organisation. *'Most people,'* says Paul, *'confuse scale with the size of the organisation. Today, parkrun is still less than 100 people. Grow impact, not the organisation.'*

Personally speaking
I ask Paul the question I'm sure a lot of people want to ask the founder of a world-renowned social business – how has it all worked out for him personally? Paul underlines that parkrun is a non-profit and, therefore, he hasn't walked away rich. Nor, indeed, has he earned as much as other employees in the organisation. He doesn't mind that, he sees it as coming with the territory. Like most social entrepreneurs, he hasn't prioritised money and measures success in other ways.

The one thing he is proudest of is that parkrun is the success it is while remaining faithful to its founding values as a community event. On this I cannot disagree. For these values are clear to me every time I pull on my trainers on a Saturday morning and head past the smiling volunteers and fellow runners to the start-line.

Key Points from Paul:
1. You have to understand your values and not deviate from these – it's very easy to compromise too much and find your vision in pieces.
2. If something is to work in lots of different places, it needs a clear and observed set of rules and values – like a franchise.
3. Scale of impact and scale of organisation are not necessarily related.
4. As a Founder, it's important to gauge the right time to go, so the organisation can mature.
5. Professional delivery of something brilliant can be done with volunteers, if you develop the right tools.

Brett Wigdortz – Founder, Teach First
www.teachfirst.org.uk @Wigdortz

'The quality of the idea is only a small part of what makes success. Ideas are relatively plentiful and easy to have. The difficult bit is the persistence, hard work and resilience required to see them through.'

Bigger than that

It seems fitting that the son and brother of New Jersey teachers ended up as Founder-CEO of Teach First. But things are not quite that simple. For Brett Wigdortz has never stood in front of a class as a teacher. And Teach First is about far more than attracting 1,500 of the UK's smartest young graduates into teaching each year.

In Brett's own words, *'Teach First is a movement to make sure no child's educational success is held back by their socioeconomic background.'* The job of the organisation is to build a generation of leaders to spearhead this social change.

> **TEACH FIRST**
> - Teach First develops leaders in schools, helps young people decide their future, encourages innovation in education and builds a movement for change
> - The organisation partners with schools serving low-income communities in every region of England and Wales
> - Brett Wigdortz set up Teach First in 2002, has since recruited nearly 7,000 teachers and taught more than 1 million pupils in low income communities.

The click inside

Like many social entrepreneurs, Brett's story is unconventional. Let's spool back to 2001. Brett was 27. He'd been in the UK for six months with his firm McKinsey working on a seminal project called 'The War for Talent' – all about how firms compete for and keep the best people. On the back of that, Brett was part of a McKinsey team asked by HRH the Prince of Wales to look at leadership in the school system in London.

Shortly after, Brett was to visit a west London 'sink' school. He found it depressing, devoid of energy. And he was told by demoralised teachers that kids from the school could never expect to achieve top grades or go on to top universities.

Something clicked inside. Brett decided very quickly that something had to be done to create more leaders in the education system.

Brett then took a six-month leave of absence from McKinsey to design Teach First. The idea that came out was pretty simple: place thousands of top graduates into classrooms for an initial two years and support this cohort to influence the system throughout their careers.

Sometimes it helps not to know the obstacles you face
Normal today, the Teach First idea was pretty radical back when it all started. Teach First graduates would skip formal teacher-training college for a year and, after a short induction, go straight into the classroom. They would be in at the deep end in some of Britain's roughest schools.

While Brett found support for Teach First in many quarters, the practicalities of bringing something new into life at scale were extremely challenging. Brett's personal circumstances both helped and hindered. He was young, *'immature'* in his own words. He was an American immigrant, so he didn't know the British culture yet. Bizarrely, Brett was a management consultant who hadn't yet managed a team. And he knew hardly anybody in education.

These potential handicaps were offset by the fact that Brett could approach an old problem with new eyes. *'I had determination, naiveté, I didn't give up easily, I was good at bringing people around me, getting the skills together, building a strong team.'*

Brett quickly built a coalition of support that, after less than two years, saw the first Teach First cohort of 200 recruits signed off by Ministers. From here, Teach First grew dramatically. The Teach First Alumni, 15 years in, number over 7,000.

Role model
Teach First now has its first Member of Parliament and a

Number 10 policy adviser, both from early intakes. It has spawned similar initiatives in policing (Police Now), social work (Frontline) and prisons (Unlocked Graduates). Now, Brett is passing the torch to a new CEO. Unlike many of his peers now earning megabucks in consulting, he can look back and see the difference he has made. *'And they ask me why I am so happy when they are miserable in their jobs,'* he tells me, laughing.

Brett's story holds a few important and powerful lessons for future social sector leaders. The first is the importance of persistence. He talks vividly about the many 'Valleys of Death' he has experienced, where he nearly gave up on Teach First. In 2002, a Minister of State gave Teach First a definitive 'No'. Depressed and about to throw in the towel, Brett was turned around by a mentor who told him to get back to the task. He did and, a few months later, that same Minister, Stephen Timms MP, signed off. Teach First has never looked back.

A good mentor can help you see things in different ways
The second point Brett makes is the importance to him of other people: his top teams and his mentors. As a younger man, he struggled to see why people around him might not be as self-motivated and self-directed as he was.

'People management is difficult for me. I see a goal; I think people should just get us there. I didn't always prioritize the management support needed. I have been sometimes too ambitious when we may have achieved more if I had taken my foot off the gas. But it's a fine line, always.'

On mentors, Brett works closely with a FTSE 100 CEO who is also helping his transition into the next chapter of his personal journey beyond Teach First.

Further to this, Brett is part of a network of CEOs mostly from the private sector. This didn't surprise me. Brett has always worked very comfortably across sectors, more so than many social entrepreneurs and charity chiefs.

You have to see opportunities where others see threats
The third take-away lesson from meeting Brett is the scope of his vision and ambition. He sees a world of future possibilities for the social sector. This isn't based just on his upbeat disposition, but on a set of thoughtfully developed views about how the world is developing. *'Change and innovation,'* he says, *'is moving so quickly in every field as to make it very difficult indeed now to fully understand what is, in totality, actually going on.'*

The social sector, he says, will likewise have to change if society is to succeed. This is where Brett feels that opportunities will lie for new organisations that pioneer wholly novel approaches. He is undeterred by the obduracy of public service systems. Brett thinks these will be forced to change as politics responds, belatedly, to the pressures on it made manifest by Brexit and the rise of populism across advanced democracies.

With careful support, Millennials really can change the world
Like many of the leaders profiled in this book, Brett deals extensively with 'Millennials' – people born between the early 1980s and early 2000s – who form the bulk of each Teach First cohort – and many of his core leadership team.

On balance, he finds Millennials inspiring. *'The difference,'* he says, is that they are *'self-directed, looking for impact, autonomy and self-expression, less concerned with role, hierarchy or seniority.'* It does, Brett notes, require a different style of management than the traditional command-and-control – *'more like herding cats!'* he says, smiling.

Staying happy
When Brett started, he wasn't married, didn't have kids. He could work all the time, indeed had to. Today he says, *'I have a family and some hard and fast rules I stick to. So, on Fridays, I get home early, the phone is turned off till Sunday evening. In the week, I work all day and am out most evenings.'*

While Brett strikes me as more American than British in his work-ethic, I can see how it works for him. He is clearly happy on it.

On the 'lonely at the top' issue, Brett is sanguine. *'A certain amount of isolation,'* he says, *'comes with the territory. You only do this job if you can cope with that,'* he opines. He tends to agree with the view of his mentor, who runs a FTSE 100 company, that people who do the CEO role are, *'a bit weird,'* and are quite different to the norm. As time has passed, Brett has learned to embrace this part of himself, even though not everyone has always found him easy.

Finally, I ask Brett what he sees as his best advice to future social leaders. He is quick to reply. *'There is a real entrepreneurial spirit in Britain today. We live in a disruptive age. It's a great time to be an entrepreneur. Just about anything being done is going to be done differently in 10 years' time. It's an exciting time.'*

Key Points from Brett:

1. Persistence – getting through the 'Valleys of Death' is the key to any long-term change.
2. You can never do it on your own. You need lots of other people: a team, a network and great mentors.
3. Change generally is moving faster than we can fully understand – this creates lots of opportunities for brand new social purpose organisations.
4. Millennials are great to have in your organisation, but recognise they need a different type of management if you are to get the most from them.
5. Finding your own balance is key – time away from the phone and work is critical. But accept that stress and loneliness are part of the territory in any top job.

Sam Conniff,
Co-founder and Chief Purpose Officer,
Livity www.livity.co.uk @SamConiff

'One thing is certain. What got you here won't get you there.'

Just this year
This is a big year for Sam Conniff. He's soon to publish *'Be More Pirate'*, a 21st century survival guide for young leaders based on the successful strategies of 18th century pirates. His wife is expecting their second child. And it will be almost a year since handing on day-to-day control of Livity, the marketing company he co-founded 16 years ago, to a new Chief Executive.

I stride up the stairs to the reception of Livity's vast loft-style offices in Brixton. I double-take and realise it's Sam on the desk today, headset on. True to form, Sam is not where you expect to see him. We then amble past banks of Apple Macs, where groups of young people who come into Livity every day are working on their projects. *'The deal here is that, as long as they are working, young people can use this place.'*

LIVITY
- When they set up Livity in 2001, Sam Conniff and Michelle Morgan envisaged a youth marketing business agency that also helped young people at risk
- Today, in its own words, Livity is a youth-led creative network that exists to help young people change the world
- After 16 years, founder Sam has finally handed over control to a new Chief Exec.

New model

Livity, as you are probably already working out, isn't an ordinary marketing agency.

The Livity model was to connect big brands looking to sell to young people with streetwise 15–24-year-olds coming into Livity from the estates of South London. Everyone would win: young people would work on real-life marketing projects, firms like Red Bull and Topman would get distinctive new campaigns – and Livity would become a successful business.

Except that wasn't how it all panned out at first.

'I was trying to do the social entrepreneur saviour-of-the-world thing,' Sam tells me. *'I was attending court with people, chasing them down the streets if they weren't here.'*

Unsurprisingly, with Sam in social worker mode, the business side of things didn't go as well as it needed to. Sam found himself trapped in a 'seesaw' mentality of either the business going well or meeting a social mission. It always seemed to be a choice.

Things went on like this for some years, with Sam working ever harder and the pressure building up as the business grew. Sam was now in his 30s and well out of the start-up phase. Livity got better, the chaos subsided, Sam focused more on the commercial side – but Livity still struggled to balance its various aims.

Love changes everything
Things began to change quite profoundly for Sam – and Livity – when he fell in love with the woman he went on to marry.

He started to practise mindfulness and saw a therapist to help him understand his own unresolved issues. All of this enabled him to understand better what was really going on: *'Like a lot of people in social enterprise, I was hiding – using what I was doing to resolve some of my own issues – in my case, being the father I hadn't really had, to these young people.'*

Proper model
Now, Sam could decisively reposition himself and the direction of the business. He realised he was wrong to view his social business as one part doing good, the other commercial. Rather than be in conflict, these two dimensions must come into a single successful business model that included measurable impact.

This insight transformed Livity's own fortunes, as the organisation grew to 120 people and an overseas office.

Change at the top
Sam's life was changing, too. By now, he was married, a father himself and approaching 40, which is deemed elderly in the world of youth marketing.

Both for himself and for Livity, he felt it important to install new leadership. *'Founder-syndrome is real,'* he tells me. *'It's incumbent on any founder to ask if they are the right person to take things to the next level.'*

Transition out of Livity has seen Sam leave the Executive team and a long-time senior manager appointed as CEO. *'My shadow mustn't fall on her decisions,'* Sam adds. *'The most grown up thing I have ever done is to allow someone else to run this business.'* He now meets the new CEO for coffee once a week and remains on the Board. Physically in the business only a few days a week, Sam is now writing his new book and mentoring young entrepreneurs.

Lessons of leadership
What has Sam Conniff learned about social leadership? The first lesson is about taking yourself into unusual places. Sam is in reception quite deliberately when I arrive. He wants to observe people as they come and go. For him, leadership is about avoiding the routines of the boardroom and exposing yourself to wider influences.

He recalls one weekend a few years ago when he went down to Livity's office and happened across two young men who didn't know who he was. They got chatting and the two lads told him everything they thought about Livity, warts and all. While some of this was really difficult for Sam – he stayed incognito – he describes it as, *'one of my most valuable recent experiences as a CEO – because, when does anyone ever tell you the truth about your business?'*

The second lesson is about avoiding procrastination. Sam claims to find the same things difficult that every CEO does*: 'screwing up projects, negotiating the money with clients and letting people go.'* As a younger man, *'failure felt like death,'* so he tended at times to avoid dealing with difficult issues, letting them multiply. But all this gets a lot harder and scarier if you put it off: *'The second you begin the hard conversation the fear is gone.'*

Sam's final lesson is that we have to understand that the younger generation views social leadership in very different terms than we did. *'They know and feel the danger ahead better than us. And they think we have screwed it up.'*

Consequently, he says, *'many young people see making an impact as something they want to build into whatever they are doing, whether it's forming a business or whatever.'* They don't categorise in the way we do, he tells me.

Therefore, Sam says, *'we need to understand that social leadership can come from many places and not to draw the bridge around a tight and tiny group of organisations.'*

Sam's big take-away point for social leaders is about adaptation, remaining open but, most importantly, knowing yourself and understanding your motivations. *'I am not the first social entrepreneur with saviour issues,'* he says, *'nor will I be the last.'*

Key Points from Sam:
1. Try to understand your deeper motivations and ask yourself whether these are having a positive or negative effect on the way you lead.
2. What got you here won't get you there – as a social leader, avoid the assumption that future success means carrying on in the same way.
3. Social business is about developing a brilliant business that has social impact built into its business model.
4. As a social leader, put yourself in unexpected places from where you can learn.
5. The next generation does not tend to see the world in boxes, so we need a more inclusive vision of social leadership.

SECTION THREE

DIGITAL LEADERSHIP

'People's lived experience is now digital in many walks of their lives, even when dealing with parts of the state. And this is moving faster than many social sector organisations' own business models.'

Karl Wilding, Director of Policy & Volunteering, NCVO

Introduction

In most areas of life, our transactions are increasingly digital. Whether it's finding a relationship, opening a bank account or paying our taxes – it's all now online.

By and large, the social sector hasn't moved anywhere nearly as fast. Delivery is often similar to how it's always been, regardless of the fact that most people – including the poor and vulnerable – now live on their phones.

The barriers to going digital are numerous, not least the one-off costs of moving to a new channel and the implications this has for existing services. Plus, there are many in need who are also digitally excluded. The fact remains that the social sector has been slow off the mark.

Which is why we showcase some really interesting examples of digital leadership: from the RaspberryPi Foundation, led by CEO **Philip Colligan**; to **Fiona Nielsen's** Repositive; and **Zoe Peden's** Iris Speaks. All of these have created new social businesses using digital technology as the building block.

If you're still an 'analogue' organisation, what's the key to successful digital leadership? Look back, perhaps, at **Chris Sherwood** of Relate (pp 21 - 26). Its challenge was that some people who might otherwise come to Relate were going to other providers offering services via smartphones.

Things get truly intriguing with digital when you look at the newer organisations. From Cambridge, the tech team at RaspberryPi Foundation (RPF) supports the activities of thousands of coding groups for kids all over the world – from the wealthy boroughs of New York City to the poor villages of rural Romania.

In another part of Cambridge, 20 or so people at social business Repositive, are using a 'digital platform' to link research scientists and large pharmaceutical companies around the world. By digitally curating data, they are helping to create life-saving technologies.

Zoe Peden, of Iris Speaks, is also creating a 'platform'-type digital business model. She's confident that, within a few years, it will be possible to offer a free speech-therapy service for kids across the whole globe using avatars and 'bots' overseen by just a handful of people.

Digital delivery then offers possibilities for social impact at relatively low cost that could have a huge impact on the wider social sector.

Leadership in this area is tough. Making the case for digital innovation is not always easy when business as usual can be disrupted. Envisioning the kind of change that digital technologies could bring is difficult, especially when moving off an old way of doing things. Figuring out business models this might require is hard. Digital approaches are never cheap and suck up lots of money before a single penny is generated. Investors are required so ideas need also to be profitable. And the talent needed to make digital happen is scarce.

All social sector organisations find digital hard. Therefore, carrying on, in the face of this, when resources are tight and scepticism may be high, is a big digital leadership test.

Zoe Peden, Founder, Insane Logic and Iris Speaks www.irisspeaks.com @zoepeden

'You can develop and change, almost beyond recognition, from your earlier self.'

A brand new way
I meet Zoe Peden in the smart study of the Royal Society of Arts in London. Zoe is waiting for me, always early, her big smile radiating as I rush in, always late.

Zoe is a social innovator and entrepreneur. Her 'eureka moment' came when she watched Steve Jobs unveil the iPad in 2007, live on *BBC News*. Zoe was working at the time at the Makaton Charity. Instantly, she realised she could use this new device to create a new way for disabled kids to learn Makaton, which uses signs and symbols instead of speech. But the iPad had yet to hit the UK. Within 24 hours, Zoe was in New York, at the Apple Store, buying as many iPads as she could afford.

Taking the risk

Back in the UK, Zoe had some negotiation to do. To develop her idea, she knew she'd need both time and money. On top, she needed the rights to use Makaton, which resided with her employer. A deal was done over the following months, with Zoe's boss freeing her to develop what became 'MyChoicePad' – but at Zoe's own cost and risk!

For the next two years, Zoe lived off very little and put every penny she had into her idea. Progress was good, but not fast enough. Zoe's cash was about to run out when she won one of 25 Big Venture Challenge Awards from UnLtd. Not only did this offer cash, but also the connections Zoe needed to take MyChoicePad to market.

Selling the product

Now Zoe could build her company – which she called 'Insane Logic' – and a team to start selling the product. MyChoicePad started selling on day one and hasn't stopped since.

Insane Logic was evolving, too, and Zoe realised quickly the need to keep improving the offer. So, she joined a business 'accelerator' and took investment from a social investor (ClearlySo).

Growing

A few years in, success kept coming and sales kept growing, but it became clear to Zoe that, if MyChoicePad was to hit its potential, it needed the reach of a much bigger company. Plus, it just wasn't possible to raise the necessary funds herself. So, in 2016, Zoe sold Insane Logic to one of her investors. In her own words: *'Being bought out meant disappointment, dream torn apart – but also a move on to new things.'*

During the handover period, Zoe was hard at work on new venture, 'Iris Speaks'. Inspired by the Greek goddess for communication, Zoe's new company aims to open up speech and language therapy to any child who needs it, anywhere, using a variety of online technologies.

IRIS SPEAKS
- Iris Speaks provides UK-wide, family focused speech and language therapy
- The company's mission is to increase the accessibility and effectiveness of speech and language therapy using technology with a human touch
- Zoe Peden, now MD of Iris Speaks, is a multiple award-winning technology entrepreneur who has spent the last decade building products and software businesses in the field of speech and language therapy.

Addressing a market failure

Iris Speaks addresses a market failure: '*At the moment, getting this therapy is really difficult and kids wait a long time – Iris Speaks gets them what they need much quicker.*'

Right now, Iris Speaks is a paid for, private service. About this fact, Zoe has some difficult feelings (she believes in the NHS) but realises that, in the absence of any NHS buyers (far too slow), she has to go where the money is. And that is private customers stuck on an NHS waiting list who want a convenient and economic solution for their child.

Zoe's long-term vision is to offer a universal service for free, which she thinks will soon be possible with advances in speech and language therapy technologies. And, as a social entrepreneur, it is this vision which most animates her.

The road to a vision
Born in Stockport, Greater Manchester, Zoe grew up in a single parent family. *'Being brought up with a plastic spoon in my mouth: free school meals, not 'poor', but struggling,'* gave her a lot of drive. She did exceptionally well at school and just missed out on Oxbridge, ending up instead at the London School of Economics where she studied History.

But these were not happy years for Zoe. Her confidence wasn't high and she found herself surrounded by well-to-do people who were no brighter than her but far were more articulate and connected. Leaving university, she stayed in London with big dreams but struggled to be coherent in interviews, which, she says, *'is amazing considering all I do now is talk to people.'*

Zoe eventually found work in the publishing sector. Then, in the early 2000s, she got seriously interested in the internet and started building websites. Career-wise, this was a highly useful skill – yet she remained unfulfilled. Following a year off travelling, Zoe took the job with The Makaton Charity, where she struck up a powerful, developmental relationship with its CEO, Lysa Schwartz, who remains a close friend today.

Private route
A noticeable feature of Zoe's story is the route she took with her idea. Like both Sam Conniff (pp 46-51) and Fiona Nielsen (pp 73-78), Zoe decided very early to go down a private route to creation of social impact, rather than set up a non-profit venture.

For Zoe, this was very simply because the resources were not there to develop either MyChoicePad (or her next venture, Iris Speaks) from charitable or public funds.

'These products are expensive to develop, high risk and take a long time – up to a decade – to really mature, and only private investors are able to really work like that.'

This said, Zoe is keen, with Iris Speaks, to take greater care over when she involves investors. *'Once investors are on-board, you are working for them and you lose the autonomy you thought you would get as an entrepreneur.'*

Personal rewards

One of the questions you might be asking is whether MyChoicePad has made Zoe rich? The answer is no. By the time of sale, Zoe's ownership share level had already shrunk to a fraction. About this, Zoe is completely comfortable. She doubts MyChoicePad could have happened any other way. But she is happy. *'The more product I could sell, the more impact it could have and MyChoicePad was a high impact product.'*

The learning here is that younger people coming through, like Zoe, are not just joining charities or Community Interest Companies to make their life's work, but are also forming companies and working with a range of investors.

Zoe herself has learned a good deal from her journey. Perhaps the most powerful lesson has been *'that you can develop and change, almost beyond recognition, from your earlier self.'* Zoe describes herself in her 20s as *'shy, angry, introverted, completely not the person I am now.'*

Zoe puts her personal transformation down to three things. The first was a deep desire to move beyond her limitations. This involved some major changes in her late 20s while still in a conventional career: *'a move into the voluntary sector, a year out and, sadly, a divorce.'*

The second was a conscious attempt to create a powerful network around herself. *'I have this force-field now of brilliant people around me – and this is absolutely critical to how I operate.'*

Chief juggler

Zoe has also learned to look after herself better. *'In start-up world,'* she tells me, *'there is a lot of free alcohol and unhealthy food.'* Today, she has traded Pot Noodles for spinach smoothies and daily workouts in her quest for energy and longevity. Like many social sector leaders, Zoe has become conscious of lifestyle factors in long-term success. She's emphatic about the need to build yourself up: *'Believe in yourself, do look at your network, join programmes, keep your focus, treat your networking like a business.'*

Zoe's story and my own intersect at many points – the plastic spoon, the escape to university, the early lack of confidence, attracting investors, successful social venture followed by exit and new start-up around age 40. The serious learning here is that successful social leadership, of the sort Zoe has delivered, is a long-game requiring powerful networks and alliances.

And, of course, never giving up.

Key Points from Zoe:
1. **Successful social leadership comes in many forms, including private ventures.**

2. Digital when got right is a brilliant tool for social impact
   – as its costs are low.
3. Sometimes, the risk involved in social innovation cannot
   be easily funded by charities, so private investors need to
   be brought on board.
4. It's possible to change quite profoundly as a person as you
   move from 20s into 30s and beyond. Never underestimate
   your own 'power to change'.
5. Networks and alliances are absolutely pivotal to any
   successful social sector leader.

Philip Colligan,
CEO, Raspberry Pi Foundation
www.raspberrypi.org @philipcolligan

'Getting that balance right between saying, "This is the plan, we stick with it", and, "Hey, that's a fantastic idea, let's go with that", is a constant tension.'

The Raspberry Pi computer
'One of the most remarkable things about the Raspberry Pi Foundation', says Philip Colligan, CEO, *'is that we are a charity that owns a successful computer company.'*

The computer company in question – Raspberry Pi Trading Limited – produces the Raspberry Pi. About the size of a credit card and priced at $35, it's a remarkably powerful computer used in education, by hobbyists, and increasingly in industry. Fifteen million units have been shipped so far, including two to the International Space Station, where Tim Peake, the British ESA astronaut, ran programs and experiments coded by UK schoolchildren.

So, how did this all happen? In 2008, a group of computer scientists and engineers at Cambridge University, wrestling with the challenge of how to get more young people interested in studying computer science, came up with the idea of creating a low-cost programmable computer. Led by engineer and entrepreneur Dr Eben Upton, the team launched the first device in 2012, expecting to sell a few thousand units. It sold hundreds of thousands on the first day. But rather than enrich themselves, the co-founders decided early on to establish the whole venture as a charitable Foundation.

RASPBERRY PI FOUNDATION
- Raspberry Pi Foundation is the charity that owns 100% of the shares in Raspberry Pi Trading Limited, the company that produces the Raspberry Pi computer
- The company has now sold 15 million units with all profits donated to its parent charity
- The Foundation has a mission to help people all over the world learn how to make things with computers.

A shaved head

The Raspberry Pi Foundation's Chief Executive is Philip Colligan. Brought in when the company employed fewer than 30 people, in just two years Philip had already grown the team to well over 100, as Raspberry Pi spreads to all corners of the world.

Philip bristles with enthusiasm about the learning network the Foundation is putting in place across the world. '*Last week, I met a young girl from rural Romania who attends one of our CoderDojos. She had hacked a Raspberry Pi and a brain sensor to drive a robot using my brain signals!'* This was helped, the girl assured him, by the fact of his shaved head!

From tool to teacher
If the Raspberry Pi is the tool, the Foundation is the teacher. But not in any traditional sense. Raspberry Pi is not interested in rules and formalities in its coding clubs, of which over 10,000 now exist across the world.

There are no qualifications, exams or fixed-in-stone curricula. Just kids who want to learn, a load of high-quality online resources, and volunteers – often passionate programmers and engineers who want to support the next generation.

Importantly, *'The only rule is, be cool,'* Philip tells me, smiling.

No history
If the traditional charity – with its formality, processes and deep sense of history – sits at one end of the spectrum, Raspberry Pi Foundation is to be found at the other. The organisation's Cambridge HQ feels more like a technology start-up with bright young things everywhere and a real sense of possibility.

One of Philip's jobs, as a relatively new CEO, is to get the most out of this very special eco-system, while also building an organisation with global reach and influence. He has gone about this by developing partnerships, which in two cases have led to a merger.

One of these is Code Club, a UK-based charity that runs the world's largest network of after school coding clubs. The other is the CoderDojo Foundation, an Irish charity that supports over 1,000 evening and weekend computing clubs around the world. Bringing together what were effectively three start-up organisations has meant that they can invest in the back office and processing systems that are powering growth.

On brand
Philip has deliberately nurtured the Code Club and CoderDojo brands – in no small part because of the sense of community and commitment they engender.

One of Philip's largest challenges, however, in a very creative and decentralised organisation, has been developing a coherent plan that moves the Foundation's mission forward at velocity.

'*Getting that balance right between saying, this is the plan, we stick with it and, hey, that's a fantastic idea, let's go with that, is a constant tension,*' he explains. '*You don't ever want to sit on a person's creativity, but, I am conscious, at times, that I need to focus that creativity on the plan,*' he tells me.

With people
Similar questions face Philip as they do any other social sector leader. How do I take people with me? How do I find the people I really need? How do I know I am making an impact?

That last question is particularly taxing for Philip. Unlike Facebook or Google, Raspberry Pi Foundation does not demand that people surrender their data when using their systems. All of their educational resources are free and open. That means that while they know that millions of people have accessed their online learning resources this year, it's much harder to know what they did with them. To harvest personal data would, Philip says, be against the values of the community of users. So he has to find other ways to understand and report impact, including investing in a significant research programme.

Back then

How did Philip Colligan come to be where he is today? Born in the north Wales town of Rhyl, Philip's early life wasn't always easy and he ended up living away from his parents at a young age. He left school at 16 with a handful of GCSEs and spent the next few years working in a record shop and as a DJ in clubs.

It was when the owner of the record shop told Philip he would sack him if he didn't go to college that Philip enrolled at night school, which led him to Liverpool University to study law. After graduation, he entered the Civil Service Fast Stream and quickly progressed to a senior role in the Home Office, leaving in 2004 to become Assistant CEO of Camden Council while still in his early 30s.

Onto CEO

From Camden to Nesta, where Philip served as Deputy CEO. Here he helped establish the Behavioural Insights Team as a joint venture with the Cabinet Office, which has gone on to become a global success. Raspberry Pi was his first CEO job, and also his first job in Cambridge, where he lives with his partner and two children.

Despite his high-powered CV, Philip still felt a sense of trepidation when he first became a CEO: *'Nothing quite exposes you in the same way,'* he told me.

Thankfully, there have been plenty of mentors, to whom he regularly turns to for advice. Philip feels a deep sense of gratitude not only to these individuals but people in his past who have had a decisive influence, including the CEO of Camden Council, Moira Gibb and, yes, the manager of the record shop who he personally thanked on a visit back home a few years ago.

Social impact

Philip's core motivator in life is social. Or, in his words, *'to fix bits of the world that are broken.'*

He knows, as all smart people do, that beyond a certain level of income, no further happiness is to be had from money. So, beyond keeping his family comfortable, he prioritises social impact. He's fuelled by a nagging sense of under-achievement, which Philip himself attributes to his experiences of childhood. This channels into an intensity and energy that, if you have ever been around Philip, you'll find hard not to notice.

How does Philip see the future? He is clear that social enterprise organisations, like his, are going to be much more important in the future. Government, he believes, is losing its legitimacy, particularly among the young. It also lacks capacity to solve problems in a rapidly changing world. Big business is increasingly looking out of step with the needs of the future. It is businesses like Raspberry Pi *'which mobilise civil society to address social problems, that will be more important in the future.'*

Like parkrun (p32), Code Clubs and Dojos are free to use and entirely run on goodwill. The outcome, Philip believes, will be digital innovations transforming society as the kids learning to code become the innovators and entrepreneurs of the future. *'I am an optimist,'* he says with a smile.

Good advice

What is Philip's best advice to social sector leaders? He points to three things. The first is, *'Never stop learning.'* Philip is always reading, normally in batches of books on related themes – the most recent being on artificial intelligence and automation.

The second is, *'You have got to have a 'why'. You need to know your motivation.'*

The third is to look after yourself. *'Nobody wins if we burn people out – take breaks, stop, take exercise.'* The amazing Botanic Gardens in Cambridge are two minutes down the road and Philip bought a load of passes and encourages his team to go there any time for meetings, for lunch, or just to relax.

Meeting Philip and the Raspberry Pi Foundation feels like a journey into the future of our sector – informal, savvy, optimistic but also seriously ambitious about changing the world for the better.

Key Points from Philip:
1. **Raspberry Pi Foundation is a charity that owns the company that produces the Raspberry Pi – a computer that has now sold 15 million units – with a mission to help people across the world to learn how to make things with computers.**

2. There is a constant tension between a highly decentralised, creative organisation and the need to adhere to a clear long-term plan.
3. The culture and values of Raspberry Pi – open, community-led and non-traditional – are key to its success.
4. Mergers have been a key part of the growth of Raspberry Pi Foundation – but these have been genuinely beneficial to all parties.
5. Social enterprise is likely to grow as an organisational form in the future, as both government and traditional business struggle to address social challenges.

Fiona Nielsen, CEO, Repositive
www.repositive.io @repositiveio

'I don't know how companies without a social mission actually succeed. I think all companies need to be like ours.'

Better science puts people first
It was a family health crisis that propelled research-scientist Fiona Nielsen on a long journey towards setting up Repositive in 2014. While Fiona was working on a PhD, her mother was diagnosed with an advanced cancer.

Doubts that Fiona already had about her own chosen career in science were amplified. One of her deep frustrations was a 'data-disconnect' experienced on both sides of the scientific divide: researchers and companies. To explain properly, researchers doing important 'early science' often couldn't get their hands on the data they needed to do their work properly. Equally, biotech and pharmaceutical companies could not easily access this data either, slowing down progress on socially beneficial treatments.

Repositive is an attempt to bridge that gap, using a digital platform for curating available data in a form that works for both sides. Fiona: *'It's like Airbnb, in a sense, except we bring together research scientists with the data they need, and, at the same time sell access to companies to the curated data that will help them get things more quickly to clinical trials.'*

REPOSITIVE
- Repositive is a social enterprise working for efficient and ethical access to genomic data, aiming to speed up genetic diagnostics and research
- Through open science and transparent data custodianship, Repositive works. Repositive works to make a difference for patients by maximising the value of data for their benefit
- A bioinformatics scientist specialising in genome analysis, Fiona Nielsen left her job in 2013 to pursue her vision of enabling efficient genomic data sharing – first, she founded the charity DNAdigest and, a year later, Repositive, as a spin out of the charity.

Social enterprise can work
To create the kind of platform she envisaged, Fiona knew she would need significant investment – far more than trusts and foundations could ever provide.

Although she had initial reservations about setting up a private venture – *'I formerly held the view that commercial companies were evil!'* – Fiona went on Cambridge University's social innovation programme and learned about the way a social enterprise can work.

So Repositive was created as a spin-out business from a charity Fiona had initially set up called DNAdigest. But Fiona was adamant from the beginning that this had to be a mission-based organisation and that everyone in it would be hired on the basis of their full commitment to its purpose.

Repositive began small with Fiona and one other person, Adrian Alexa, who became Chief Technology Officer. To fund the early business, Fiona attracted early social investment from both UnLtd and ClearlySo, plus a number of 'angel' investors in her native Cambridge.

Becoming market-ready
The early years were about building Repositive's proposition into a solid offer to both research scientists and the commercial users of scientific research. This was primarily about showing to each side the huge benefits and savings to be made by using the new brokerage service.

Things moved very quickly from there. To be truly market-ready, Repositive had to evolve rapidly. Over a couple of years, Fiona appointed a top team comprising a number of former colleagues. To fill key positions just beyond the top team, she recruited a number of people new to the company.

Fiona finds her own role as CEO constantly changing, as new people are brought in to fill functions like marketing, communication and operations. This has freed Fiona to focus on both customers and investors.

Investors on board

Now on her third 'round' of fundraising, Fiona has brought on board a major backer in the form of Ananda Capital, a Germany-based venture capital backer with an interest in social impact, who will be joining the three investors already on Repositive's Board.

'What is it like,' I ask Fiona, 'to have investors so closely involved in the running of your business?' *'So far,'* she tells me, *'it's been really good, each investor brings a necessary specialism and, together, they've got their heads around the niche that Repositive currently occupies.'*

Added to this, all investors are aligned with the company's mission and purpose and can see how, if the company succeeds, they will see a return over the long term.

At the moment, Repositive's sales are growing fast and ahead of target. But they do not cover the costs of developing the company. Yet, in the foreseeable future, it will be possible to increase sales and impact dramatically without adding much to cost. As Fiona reminds me, this is a digital offer, *'there is no human broker.'*

The accidental entrepreneur

Fiona sees herself as something of an accidental entrepreneur. *'Five years ago, if someone had told me I would be CEO of this thing, doing all that I do now, I would not have believed it.'*

In terms of leadership style, perhaps due to her Scandinavian roots, Fiona puts a great store by team-working and collaboration. *'The best moments are when we celebrate as a team, something we do regularly.'*

Fiona believes communication and visibility to be very important and has designed her CEO role so that there is still plenty of time to spend alongside her 20 colleagues in her Cambridge HQ.

From Fiona, we can learn that it isn't always possible to take forward a social mission using conventional grants and donations. *'You have to be open to working with others who might have different drivers but enough shared ground to work with you.'* As Fiona's investors have done.

A second point might be that a social mission is a really powerful cornerstone for any company, particularly when that mission is built into the business model, as it is at Repositive. *'Whenever we help someone, we celebrate together.'*

A third is that, to survive as a Founder-CEO, you must evolve your role as the company grows. In Fiona's words: *'While I had many hats, most have now been given away.'*

Key Points from Fiona:
1. **Fiona decided, after initially setting up a charity, that a private business was the most effective way for Repositive to deliver its particular social mission.**
2. **Repositive uses digital technology to address a need in the market for brokerage between scientists and people who can use their data.**
3. **Building a mission-based organisation is, in some respects, easier than building one where profit is the overriding preoccupation.**

4. The CEO of a start-up needs to be constantly evolving their role as the venture grows.
5. With digital technology the growth of impact does not need to be matched by equivalent increases in costs.

SECTION FOUR

CULTURAL LEADERSHIP

'It's incredibly useful to take on non-executive roles and even better to use it as an opportunity to gain an insight into how other sectors operate.'

Judith Brodie, CEO, Beating Bowel Cancer

Introduction

Culture is classically defined as 'the way we do things around here'. It's actually a lot more than that. Culture encompasses not only behaviour, but also the values, beliefs and attitudes sitting behind.

In social sector organisations, culture can be a massive enabler and motivator for staff, volunteers and users alike. I recall well the first time I encountered a nurturing, supportive culture, as a young volunteer with Newcastle-based charity Skills for People in the 1990s. This spell was, in many ways, the making of me and I have tried to take some of that 'secret sauce' into my own ventures.

Culture, of course, can have the opposite effect, leading to stasis, inefficiency and, in some extreme cases, the end of the organisation. You can tell if a culture has gone bad within minutes of walking through the door.

Successful social sector leadership is about moving a culture to where it needs to be. This isn't easy. Culture moves slowly. Try to shift it too quickly and it will resist. As the leadership writer Peter Senge said, 'People don't dislike change, they dislike *being changed*. Equally, accepting all current parameters, without robust challenge, will render any attempt at change ineffective, as many of you will have found.

So what do successful social leaders do in relation to culture?

Lesley Dixon took over PSS in 2009, a charity with its roots in Victorian times and a paternalist culture of the 'great and the good' to go with it. Lesley has worked patiently over a long time to create a more egalitarian and collaborative approach with staff and users alike.

Thomas Lawson had a different kind of cultural challenge, having to rebuild Leap Confronting Conflict following a near-miss with insolvency just as he was taking over. This presented an opportunity for Thomas to create a very unique culture for the organisation that clearly mirrors Leap's own pioneering approach with young people who are involved in conflict.

For **Simon Blake** of the NUS, the cultural challenge as CEO is to balance being an enabler of a young, excited short-term student leadership, while also maintaining a stable long-term direction for his organisation.

Lesley Dixon, CEO, PSS
www.psspeople.com @lesley_dixon

'We do things with people, not for or to them.'

For a more equal world
There are some people who stand by their principles and others who simply go with the flow. Some lead change and others prefer to follow. Lesley Dixon grew up knowing that she wanted to make a difference in the world.

Her grandfather, and particularly her mother, instilled in her a strong sense of social justice. She has always been quick to champion the underdog and level life's playing field.

PSS, the charity and social business Lesley leads, was founded in 1919 by Eleanor Rathbone, a suffragette, Liverpool City Councillor and, from 1922, a Member of Parliament. Born into a privileged family, Rathbone was horrified by the poverty she saw in her home city.

'*I think*', she says, '*that, if Eleanor Rathbone were to visit the charity she founded today, she would be pleasantly surprised.*' She and Lesley Dixon share a determination to create a more equal world.

PSS
- PSS, or Person Shaped Support, is a charity founded in 1919 by a former suffragette and Liverpool City Councillor, who vowed to do something about the poverty in the city
- Today, it sits alongside Local Government and NHS services, plugging the gaps and providing 'on the ground' support for a wide array of people
- Seeing an opportunity to make a difference in the city close to where she grew up, Lesley Dixon took the post of CEO in 2009.

Getting the experience

At university, Lesley was an active member of the student union. It's also where she met her husband. Unsure of the direction she wanted her career to take when she graduated, Lesley applied for the role of Commercial Manager at a London university's student's union. '*I perhaps didn't have the experience to take on a commercial role,*' she said, '*but was successful and quickly learned the ropes.*'

The next decade saw Lesley's student union career grow as she took on bigger and bigger roles. For a time, she worked alongside Matt Hyde, now CEO of the Scout Association, also profiled in this book. But Lesley knew she would not want to work in the student union movement for ever.

The Liverpool Personal Service Society

Just after, in 2009, following a decade as Chief Executive of the Leeds University Union, Lesley secured the CEO role at Liverpool-based PSS. Just as Eleanor Rathbone had started the organisation in response to the poverty she saw at the end of the Great War, so too was Lesley aware of the huge inequalities that remain in Liverpool today.

PSS is an unusual charity; often well ahead of its time in developing new services. Legal Aid, Age UK and Relate can all trace their roots back to what was then called the 'Liverpool Personal Service Society'.

The organisation's reach has grown beyond Liverpool with teams operating in Manchester, Yorkshire, north Wales and the Midlands. Further growth is planned, but closer to home, rather than build a portfolio of isolated outposts.

If you want to involve stakeholders, use language they will understand

Lesley is keen to make sure the organisation stays bang up to date and relevant to today's needs. Yes, PSS was delivering services before the statutory sector got involved. But, as statutory services evolve, so too must the PSS offer, she tells me.

So, Lesley also sees to it that the language used within the organisation moves with the times. What many would call the 'strategic plan' is published by PSS as the 'Big Plan'. It contains big ambitions, all described in simple language with plenty of illustrations and flow charts. The PSS way is to use friendly, familiar phrases that reassure.

'We wanted everyone to be feel part of the future we're trying to create, so have used language everyone will feel comfortable with, rather than corporate jargon.'

Staying on course
Many services are co-designed with local councils. There can be fear and stigma attached to social care, particularly for older people, whose last contact with any form of social care may have been when their own parents needed help, decades earlier.

Things are very different today.

PSS has a history of making tough decisions and not bowing to pressure to change course. Lesley talks of the time, before she joined, when the Catholic Church did not approve of the family planning clinics PSS used to run. PSS lost many volunteers for a time as a result, but quickly recruited more who were unwilling to support the Church's boycott of the charity.

Of course, you can't please all the people all the time. As a leader, Lesley aims to be open and approachable, but equally when tough decisions have to be made she makes them – giving the signal that she expects this of others.

It's the little things
With more than 400 employees – only 100 of whom work at the Liverpool Head Office – Lesley could easily become remote. But she makes a point of visiting services and meeting staff. She talks passionately about how staff go the extra mile to help service users.

Borrow whatever works well and give it a go
The third sector is particularly willing to share what works

with others. Lesley networks widely and often brings
new ideas she has seen working elsewhere back to the
organisation.

On recruitment, however, Lesley is sure they already
have a system that works brilliantly. Not only do they
focus on enthusiasm rather than qualifications, but they
use friendly, rather than formal language through the
process. Job offer letters carry the phrase 'we're rooting for
you' because the business wants to see every new recruit
succeed.

Profit is good
Profit is not a dirty word at PSS. Generating trading profits
enables investment in new services and ideas. It also means
the organisation can do more for those who use their
services.

With many years' experience of being a Trustee herself,
Lesley knows that she has a good Board to both support
and at times challenge her. Her Chair is related to Eleanor
Rathbone, PSS's founder. He and the rest of the Board are
now representative of a wide cross section of society – not
always the case in the past.

How you make people feel
Lesley likes quotations. On her office door is one by Sheryl
Sandberg: *'I want every little girl who someone says they're
bossy to be told instead they have leadership skills.'*

Another favourite is by Maya Angelou: *'I've learned that
people will forget what you said; people will forget what you
did; but people will never forget how you made them feel.'*

Key Points from Lesley:

1. Taking a non-executive directorship, or becoming a Trustee, can widen your experience and equip you for your future career.

2. Hardship can spark innovation. Your challenge is to make that innovation sustainable.

3. Make your strategic plan simple, explicit and free of jargon. Make it easy for your staff, stakeholders and service users to feel committed to it.

4. Recruit people with the attitude and determination to succeed. You can teach them the skills they need to do the job.

5. The bigger your job, the more important it is to make time for yourself. Balance is key to continued success.

Thomas Lawson – CEO, Leap Confronting Conflict www.leapconfrontingconflict.org.uk @ThomasJLawson

'If we expect too much of our leaders, they will only disappoint us, I get concerned about the cult of leadership, the idea that someone at the top has all the answers and can cope with anything.'

Doubling up

I climb the stairway of a frowsy low-rise behind Finsbury Park station to be met by the wall-of-energy that is Thomas Lawson, CEO of Leap Confronting Conflict (Leap). Tom is unusual among the social leaders in this book in that he is also Chair of a £3m family retail business. Lawsons, in Devon, is run by his sister and many of the challenges there, he tells me, are just the same as those faced in a charity.

This dual role isn't the only thing that stands out about Tom. The other is his reflectiveness. About himself, but also his organisation and, specifically, how as a CEO, he tries to operate.

Somehow different

To understand Tom better, one needs to hear his story. Born into a close Quaker family on a smallholding in Devon, Tom grew up the youngest of four children. He knew early on he was different, in a way that possibly wasn't easy for his family, so didn't explore further. He went away to school and was bullied quite severely – partly, he believes, because he wasn't at that point accepting of himself. *'Kids'*, he tells me *'can spot inauthenticity a mile off.'* Then he attended a youth camp at 15, run by some brilliant people who helped Thomas understand himself: he was gay. Increasingly comfortable in himself, he returned to school – and the bullying stopped.

But then tragedy struck. At 16, he lost his beloved older brother in a car accident, a shattering event that left him deeply unhappy and his family in great distress. Fuelled at this time by a passion for social justice (*'I was an awfully self-righteous teenager'*), Tom went to the London School of Economics, majoring in international development and women's studies, then worked for a succession of organisations in the peace and social justice field, including Unicef.

Tom left there following another personal loss, the death of his boyfriend from AIDS-related cancer and joined Terrence Higgins Trust, before spending six years at NAM, the HIV information charity. Between jobs he did spells of consulting work (*'very usual for me'*) before becoming Deputy CEO at Prisoners Abroad. When the job of CEO of Leap Confronting Conflict came up in 2010, *'I had never wanted a job so badly before.'*

LEAP CONFRONTING CONFLICT
- Leap is an award-winning national youth charity that provides inspirational conflict management training and support to young people and the professionals working with them
- It supports young people aged between 11 and 25 to make changes in their lives by gaining a greater understanding of themselves and their relationship with conflict
- When Tom Lawson became CEO in 2010, he had the massive job of turning around a struggling charity and regrowing Leap as an organisation.

In at the deep end

What awaited Tom at Leap was a very tough call indeed for a first-time CEO. Income had collapsed from £1.8m to £0.4m. Government grants had pretty much stopped and the charity was very close to the wire.

By the end of that first financial year, with the support of the team of staff, trustees and chair, Patrick Dunne, the income had recovered to £1m.

The financial aspects of what was required of him, Tom found straightforward enough. But it was the people-aspects that he found challenging. *'People were really upset, understandably, and the whole SMT by that stage had gone, so I was dealing with this mostly on my own. Quite quickly, I learnt to lean on Patrick and to encourage flexibility in the team – for example, the director of finance helped out with fundraising applications.'*

Dark days, tough calls

In the few months before Tom started, the Board reduced the staff from 26 to 11 and closed all of the organisation's regional offices. All in consultation with Tom. *'When you looked under the hood, everything was difficult: senior management, IT, even the photocopier contracts.'*

It was here that Tom learned about the importance of flexibility: *'In that first year I had to constantly recalibrate my understanding of the emerging reality of the organisation.'* But, next to some of the things Thomas had gone through by a young age, this wasn't the worst. And this was something that helped him keep a perspective during the darkest days.

Still, more mistakes

Since that time, Leap's focus has sharpened – which young people it is there for and what it is there to achieve. Its finances have stabilised and turnover has doubled. This has enabled Tom to build a senior team that works well as a unit. But not without pain.

'The mistake I made as a CEO was managing the senior management team not as a team, but as individuals. Whole team meetings weren't a success. Now the team has a stronger idea of itself. When recruiting, I am now much more interested in the extent to which someone will bring a complementary difference in team character: that's the attitude to team success.'

Open with uncertainty

Tom is highly critical of the commonly held view of the heroic CEO as an all-knowing leader-figure. *'This is nonsense, damaging to the CEO and to the organisation. Every CEO benefits from an open discourse and from being able to show uncertainty.'*

Unhappiness is still a feature at times in Tom's life. He has bad days when he might choose to work from home. *'I have periods when I struggle. I don't hide this from others. Paradoxically, showing vulnerability, and my open response to it, illustrates my resilience.'*

At Leap, the ability to deal in difficult emotion is a key part of the organisation's mission. *'Conflict is an amazing opportunity,'* he says, *'but it can turn into something unmanageable. This is where the real personal development lies.'*

About Leap's work, Tom is evangelical. *'I was amazed how much self-awareness Leap's work afforded young people to grow and how it can happen so quickly.'*

More difference, please
Three other themes stood out when talking to Tom. The first is his passionate concern for greater diversity in social sector organisations.

'At Leap, 50% of staff are from black, Asian and minority groups. The value of lived-experience in the team means we make much better decisions for the young people for whom we work.' That is unusual. Diversity, he says, *'brings challenge and perspective that you just don't get if you insist on a degree from a Russell Group University.'*

Coach, rather than manager
The second theme is Tom's view of his own role as a person's manager. He sees his role almost as that of a coach, adapting his style and approach to fit the needs of the individual and the group, rather than expecting people to

fall in with him, as senior people often do. *'I have to flex,'* he says. *'If it's a big picture person, I need to adjust to that. If it's a detail person, I need to adapt to that and go from there.'* Again, this is unusual.

All for one

The third theme is an awareness that social change requires all three sectors to play a part. *'Social change is,'* Tom says, *'a three-legged stool – with business, the public sector and social sectors each with a role.'* He is an admirer of people in other sectors who see this. Like Paul Polman, CEO of Uniliver, now a 'B Corp' that has committed to cutting its carbon footprint by half while doubling its revenues. As non-exec chairman of Lawsons, a £3m business employing 75 people and making modest profits in rural Devon, Tom also knows that companies have to have values at their heart too – if they are to be sustainable.

Always inspired

I end by asking Tom who inspires him. He points to Bayard Rustin, the black American civil rights activist who was also gay. Then he points to many others: Julie Bentley of Girlguiding (p13) *'for clearly making the Guides a feminist organisation – and taking on the* Daily Mail'; the young people in Leap, who, from care and prison, go on to become leaders in their communities: Michael Young, founder of the Open University, *Which? Magazine* and the School for Social Entrepreneurs.

My take-away from Tom is that it is possible to be both vulnerable and strong as a leader. He is also as much as a coach of his team as an 'in charge' boss. His passion for social change is palpable. He leads from behind. He is distinctive – and inspiring.

Key Points from Thomas:
1. The 'hero' view of the CEO-leader does a disservice to the CEO and the organisation.
2. To be more successful, organisations need to be far more diverse.
3. To manage successfully, a CEO must facilitate the whole team, not just the individuals in it.
4. Commercial discipline is essential to any successful social sector organisation.
5. All three sectors play an important role in social change – the 'three-legged stool'.

Simon Blake, CEO, National Union of Students www.nus.org.uk @Simonablake

'Know your beliefs, know your values. Compromise on anything else, but not on those.'

New mandate

Simon Blake is one of the better-known voices in the social sector. He forged his reputation as CEO of Brook, the sexual health charity and as Chair of Compact Voice. Today he is CEO of the National Union of Students and a Trustee of the LGBT charity Stonewall.

Although the NUS have a clear social mission around the welfare of students, it isn't a typical social sector organisation, not least because it's run by students themselves.

My number one question to Simon was about what it's like having a Board where the majority of members are directly elected, often quite politicised young people who are around

96

for a maximum of two years – each keen to pursue their mandate.

To Simon's credit, he doesn't duck the question: '*You need to spend enough time with people, you need to listen, know which battles to pick – and which decisions are in your jurisdiction. And sometimes, when your advice isn't taken, you need patience.*'

Difficult job

To many people, myself included, Simon's job would feel too difficult – providing stable long-term leadership around some fixed points, while enabling the President and other officers to make a personal impact.

Simon sees the key as having a clear focus on some long-term goals that remain the same whoever is in office, and ensuring there is plenty of space for the elected leadership to make their mark.

In time terms, he delineates this in a 60/40 split between near-term and long-term objectives. The art of managing such a large moving-picture '*is to start the right number of new things and ensuring old things are set aside.*' He is clear that it isn't always easy to get the balance right.

NATIONAL UNION OF STUDENTS
- The NUS is a confederation of students' unions in the United Kingdom. Around 600 students' unions are affiliated, accounting for more than 95% of all higher and further education unions in the UK
- The organisation promotes, defends and extends the rights of 7 million students, heads up a prosperous and sustainable student movement and brings together evidence-based campaigns and student-led democracy
- In 2015, Simon Blake became CEO, looking to take the NUS forward at a difficult time for further education.

The multi-purpose organisation

NUS, to those who don't know it, is a distinctive organisation. Its membership is made up of Student Unions from Higher and Further Education. Many are large businesses in their own right, with sophisticated retail and leisure offers to rival those of the cities that surround them.

It is as a scale provider of a wide range of business and policy support to Student Unions that the NUS earns most of its income. This makes it very much a social business in terms of its income-model.

On top of this, NUS is a major events organisation (in the first three months of 2017 there were 14 democratic conferences with over 2,000 delegates). As well, it is a policy voice for students in all matters concerning education, access and, occasionally, wider political issues. NUS is the ultimate multi-purpose organisation.

Young affinity

To do this particular leadership job requires an affinity with younger people – which is a standout theme in Simon's life. He isn't sure where this comes from. He realises his affinity with the FPA and Brook sexual health charities probably traces back to his own life. Simon's older brother unintentionally (as far as Simon knows) fathered a child at 17. Simon himself came out as gay during the 1990s when AIDS was taking many younger gay men's lives.

His plan at university was to become an Educational Psychologist. This lasted until he started working during a year between undergrad and postgrad, getting a job at the Family Planning Association (FPA).

At the FPA, Simon met people who had dedicated their lives to social service and found many of them to be kindred spirits. It was here that Simon met a key mentor, Gill Frances, who went on to be his boss a few years later when he was at the Sex Education Forum. Gill taught him many of the fundamentals that helped him in his first CEO job at Brook, notably to build a strong unit around you and *'to employ people who can do the things you can't do or don't like doing'.*

Re-inventing Brook

It was at Brook that Simon made his name over a ten-year tenure. During this time, he oversaw the reinvention of Brook from a federation ('many Brooks') into a single unitary structure.

The change process was tough, he says, as there was huge attachment to individual parts of Brook, which *'meant a lot of talking, many hours spent on trains and sitting in rooms listening to people.'*

99

He thinks they got lots right and some stuff wrong. *'If there was a lesson here, we probably took too long between the decision to consolidate and finally doing it,'* he said.

In Simon's view, the case for consolidation was overwhelming. *'We were providing regulated services at scale and needed to do so in a really challenging marketplace. We also needed to provide a single voice at policy and mainstream level. Federation, while right for many organisations, just couldn't work for Brook.'*

Change for Simon came when he realised – after nearly a decade at Brook and 21 years in the sexual health sector – that he'd been saying the same things for too long. It was clear that Brook needed a fresh leader with a new vision. *'Right for Brook, right for me.'*

On struggle
Like all CEOs, Simon is able to look back on periods when it wasn't so easy or when he struggled.

One of his struggles, in common with many social sector CEOs, was being able to make a powerful enough contribution on the operational and financial sides. Simon remedied this by taking an accountancy course, but is quick to recommend that anyone taking a job in the sector gets hold of these sides of the job with both hands, especially during periods of change.

Future concerns
Simon Blake has always held strong views on the social sector. And he has some concerns, notably about the absence of the often-talked about paradigm-shift we need in the social sector right now.

'*We have to imagine the currently unimagined. We know collaboration, strong leadership and funding integration are critical. But there has to be something that radically uprates the contribution the sector could make to a future that doesn't look great.*'

What might this look like? Simon here talks about what is happening in the youth sector where CEOs are collaborating, sharing and working together beyond the immediate good of their own organisations on a level he thinks is unprecedented. '*This is all built on trust and on a shared belief in coming together for the common good.*' What this will translate into beyond the projects already in train isn't clear, but Simon is convinced, as am I, that much deeper collaboration is one of the keys to a more powerful social sector.

Marathon man

How does Simon approach his personal marathon as a CEO? One is by actually doing marathons! Each year he does at least two with a 'Personal Best' well inside four hours. Time running is his thinking time. His other big pastime is horse-riding and he co-owns a horse. Hacks in the countryside, coupled with speedy bike-rides to work, weaving through London traffic, give Simon the headspace he needs to turn up as CEO with a clear mind for the day ahead.

Like many CEOs, Simon also understands the power of rest for rebuilding and takes an annual 'health holiday' in which yoga, relaxation and massage all feature. '*No phones allowed.*' Simon's best advice to future CEOs is quite simple: '*Know your beliefs, know your values, compromise on anything else but not on those.*'

Key Points from Simon:

1. The way to handle a Board with short-term objectives is to have long-standing agreement over the longer-term strategy.
2. The case for consolidation is most powerful when there are clear capabilities needed for success that can't be created in any other way.
3. It is easy to take too much time to implement major change once it is agreed – all stakeholders prefer pace once a decision has been reached.
4. The CEO in the social sector needs a strong enough handle on financial and operational dimensions, particularly during periods of major change.
5. While adapting incrementally to its changed environment, the social sector hasn't yet made the 'paradigm shift' in its approach that many have been talking about during the decade or so following the economic crash of 2008.

SECTION FIVE

TEAM LEADERSHIP

'As CEO, I've realised I'm always giving off a message even when I don't intend to. That has been a learning curve in itself.'

Lindsay Weaver, CEO, Climb

Introduction

 As Jo Owen puts it in his excellent book, *How to Lead*, the right team is the dream team. It will turn mountains into molehills and crises into opportunities. He also points out, correctly, that if you settle for the 'B Team', you will struggle.

The reality is that as a leader, you might find yourself with a 'B Team', at least to begin with. A team chosen by a predecessor or, as featured here, a team that worked well inside the public sector, but was not fit for purpose once an independent organisation.

The leaders profiled here have all taken their teams through significant change. In all cases, to bring about success, this has meant building senior teams with the necessary capabilities, values and ways of working.

Their stories reveal some important truths about how to build teams: that skills matter, but not as much as values; that fitting people in is less important than finding the right fit; and that high performing teams need a diverse mix of people, including those very different from you, their leader.

There is also much to learn here about how to motivate a team. Clarity of vision is absolutely key to this. Knowing where you're going. But it's about what you are like with people. The care you show for them and their career. The respect you show by not micro-managing them. The thanks you offer when things go well.

Conversely, great team leadership means setting expectations, a willingness to have difficult conversations, never shading the truth and understanding that being respected matters far more than being liked. Seeking popularity means you will duck difficult calls.

So, to the leaders. **Janet Tuohy's** challenge was to take her management team from Salford Council with her to create a brand new employee-owned social business. Predictably, this was not easy as the skillsets required were different and yawning gaps emerged.

Matt Hyde's task was that, when he joined the Scout Association, it wasn't yet as socially inclusive or impactful as he or his Board wanted it to be. The challenge he successfully addressed was to construct a team that could build membership and activity in previously neglected areas to create a more modern, diverse and socially active Scout movement.

For **Kuljit Sandhu** of RISE Mutual, the task facing her resembled that of Janet, in that she was creating a new business from scratch comprising public servants, not all of whom were up for the journey. Her principal task was to construct a team that could fulfil a vision for efficiency and growth in a newly marketised criminal justice system.

Janet Tuohy, CEO, Aspire CIC
www.iamaspire.org.uk @janet_tuohy

'*I knew that that the way to succeed was to empower, encourage and support every one of our staff to feel valued.*'

Recognising the challenge
Janet Tuohy is now a Chief Executive of a £10m turnover social care business in Salford, Greater Manchester, having lived and worked in the north-west nearly all her life.

It could have all been different for Janet. Adopted as a baby by a loving family from Manchester, many of her contemporaries were among the 130,000 children sent to Australia from the UK and Ireland as young children, part of a scheme from the 1920s to 1970s to populate the nation with what was then called 'good white stock'.

And it was growing up in the north-west with a friend who

had a learning disability that encouraged Janet to follow a career in social work. As a child, Janet could never understand why her friend was sent away to a residential special school, far from family and friends while she stayed at home.

Janet's own schooling was challenging enough. Being dyslexic herself meant assumptions were made about her abilities, too. She soon realised that she had to take responsibility for making her own way in the world. This led Janet to her first job working with children and adults with learning disabilities.

Supporting vulnerable people
Apart from a short spell in the Metropolitan Police (*'I knew pretty quickly this was a mistake'*), Janet spent 30 years with Stockport and then Salford Council social services.

By 2011, it was becoming clear that government spending cuts were going to unpick most of her services. This hurt. In preceding years, Janet's services had become increasingly innovative, for example, mixing people with different types of vulnerability in a single care setting. It worked. Everyone benefited.

Mutual satisfaction
Then she heard from a friend about the possibility of spinning out from the Council as a Public Service Mutual. In 2015, Janet led her organisation from the familiar home of the Council into a new world as a Public Service Mutual.

She was glad she did. By now, funding cuts were starting to mean that only those with greatest need could be supported.

This did not sit comfortably with Janet's belief that early intervention is more cost effective than acting only when people reach crisis. She was glad of the opportunity now available to do things differently.

ASPIRE CIC
- Aspire for Intelligent Care and Support CIC supports adults and young people with complex needs, learning disabilities, physical disabilities and older people in Salford and beyond
- A community interest company limited by shares, Aspire is employee-owned, with everyone entitled to buy a £1 share after six months' service
- Already Head of Social Services at Salford City Council, Janet Tuohy has led Aspire since 2015 in its early years as a social enterprise.

But the culture-change Janet wanted to create was massive. Aspire was to go from public ownership to staff ownership. The Council was to have no shares in Aspire, nor seats on the Board. Employee shareholders would elect one of their number to sit on the Board. The business was to be a living wage employer – no small thing in a sector dominated by care workers paid minimum wage.

New culture vs old culture
Culturally, Janet wanted an organisation that was good at listening and responding to its service users and their families. She wanted innovation and a can-do, will-do approach from everyone.

109

To get this, Janet says, she had to make people feel secure: *'To have a conversation about the change you want to see, you've got to first deal with the natural worries people are going to have about their own situations.'*

So, earning a hearing, meant dealing first with the terms and conditions of employees transferring into Aspire from the Council. Most painfully for the business, this meant taking on the cost and future liability for public sector pensions.

This opened the door, however, for serious conversations with managers and staff about how Aspire was to be different and for Janet to set expectations afresh.

'This included a shift from a Council dependency-culture to a commercial culture,' Janet asserts. *'Part of the problem,'* she says, *'was that people had been protected for many years from any kind of pressure around commerciality and we had to say to people – if this business isn't as successful as any other care company, we go under.'*

But progress was slow. *'There were many conversations and meetings, but little by way of new business,'* she told me. Part of the challenge was that her entire senior management team had all come with her, none of whom had worked in a commercial setting before.

Janet realised that it would take more than a re-badging of senior managers and exhortation from her to create a more commercial culture. So, she re-designated the senior colleague whose brief had included business-development and looked outside instead, to the market.

Building on confidence
In April 2017, Janet appointed a new Business Development Director from outside the new organisation.

'This is giving the organisation fresh impetus and forging new relationships – and generating a commercial atmosphere.'

Culturally, Janet also encouraged the development of new services, often suggested by front-line staff or service users themselves, using small grants: *'This is how the "Our Sound" choir came about. Singing together is a great way to make new friends and build self-esteem.'*

While the choir is unlikely to ever release a CD, it now has 20 members and is changing lives.

Growing leaders
Janet is aware that culture change does not happen that quickly. Yet she also knows the truth in the dictum *'Show me the leader, show me the culture'*. While aware that it will be years, possibly, before everyone in the Aspire workforce is operating according to the same values, she is conscious that she has to model and make clear what she wants.

Culturally, the move to mutualisation is one of moving power to and then through an organisation. Delegation and handing responsibility down is all management textbook stuff. But, with letting go comes an unavoidable sense of loss. Now, Janet sees her senior managers experience that same feeling of loss, as they in turn delegate what once she delegated to them. *'It's how you grow an organisation. It's also how you grow as a leader,'* she says, plaintively.

Key Points from Janet:

1. Our early lives do shape our attitudes and focus our ambition. To what extent has your choice of career path been shaped by your early experiences?

2. Good ideas are as likely to emerge at the coalface as in the Boardroom. Do your staff feel that their ideas will be taken seriously and perhaps be acted upon?

3. As a Public Service mutual, you can create new partnerships in ways that just are not possible when within a Council. How soon will you wait before you start to knock on new doors?

4. Big change happens when lots of small changes take place. Are you waiting for something big to happen, or improving what is within your reach right now?

5. Delegating can be painful, but letting go is an essential part of leading a growing and evolving organisation. Are you clinging on to things you should be passing on to others?

Matt Hyde, CEO, The Scout Association
www.scouts.org.uk @matthyde

'You have to keep evolving and adapting the organisation and its offer, to stay current, relevant and sustainable.'

Community minded
In 1876, Matt Hyde's great great-grandfather started a retail business in the Cambridgeshire Fens. The nature of trade in those days meant that the family became involved with all aspects of community life.

So, it was no surprise that Matt grew up getting involved with things too. He joined the Scouts and later got involved in running his local Troop. He did well at school and went to university to study English. And he got involved with things here too, captaining the football club and running for election to the Students' Union.

THE SCOUT ASSOCIATION
- The Scout Association is a federated charity that has provided comprehensive support to local Scouting charities in the UK since 1907, when Robert Baden-Powell founded the organisation
- Today there are more than 457,000 youth members (boys and girls) supported by more than 154,000 adult volunteers; a further 51,000 young people are waiting for a place
- A boy scout in his youth, Matt Hyde rejoined as CEO in 2013, immediately making an impact in his determination to grow the membership organisation.

Student leader

At the age of 23, Matt was elected President of the University of London Union, leading 100,000 students across the university's many colleges.

This role introduced Matt to the business of running a membership organisation. From the way he still talks about it, I can see he found this fascinating. It was perhaps no surprise to see him move from an elected role to being appointed to manage one of its constituent student unions at Kings College London and then Goldsmiths. And, ultimately, for him to become Chief Executive of the National Union of Students.

At NUS Matt was now managing a confederation of student unions with 7 million members and an annual turnover of more than £70m. This was business on a very different scale to the family firm started by his ancestor some 130 years earlier.

'I think community involvement is in my genes, though I don't think my forebears could have imagined the complexity of organisations I've found myself running.'

More strategic, more political, more networked

While running the National Union of Students (NUS), Matt also found time to complete a part-time MBA which he found useful as his role became increasingly strategic. His network expanded, inevitably becoming more political. Just as Matt's career has moved rapidly, so too have the careers of some of his NUS contemporaries. His address book contains senior politicians from both sides of the House of Commons.

Back to his future

In April 2013, Matt took the opportunity to apply his experience and considerable enthusiasm in a new role, joining the Scout Association as Chief Executive.

Deriving income from commercial services as well as charitable activity, the Scout Association is similar to the NUS in many ways. Matt regularly meets with CEOs of other UK federated charities to discuss common challenges. It's another useful network. *'It doesn't matter that our federations all do different things,'* he says, *'because the way things are done can be surprisingly similar.'*

It is no mean feat to continue to grow a youth organisation in today's busy world. Recruiting volunteers is not easy. There are now more alternative ways to spend your free time. Matt himself is a volunteer Cub Scout leader in the town where he lives. Like many others, he simply cannot commit to be free on the same evening every week. *'Flexibility is key to any volunteering opportunity,'* he smiles.

Transforming the Scouts

Many will have viewed Scouting as a white middle-class pursuit. While that's never been totally true, it's a perception Matt has been keen to change since his appointment.

To this end, over the past three years, Scouting has started up in 460 new areas of deprivation. This is the result of its strategy *Scouting For All* that commits members to embrace young people with disabilities, from ethnic minority groups and of all sexual orientations. 27% of scouts today are girls and women.

This has all been in a fast-changing context around safeguarding. This takes a lot of Matt's time. *'Safety is our number one priority,'* Matt explained, *'we want people to have fun, enjoy adventure and develop skills for life but we have a duty to parents and young people that they can undertake activities safely.'*

Matt is also keen to keep Scouting bang up to date. Older Explorer Scouts can gain valuable CV enhancing experiences, including, for example, Duke of Edinburgh Awards. As Matt knows from his experience, recruiters are looking for people who've engaged with the world, rather than just amassed academic qualifications.

Today's community mind

Matt recognises the importance of being involved with the charity sector debate. With statutory funding in decline, the sector is in a tough place. Matt is currently deputy chair of NCVO and so engaged in the national conversation about how tomorrow's need can be best met. He describes his NCVO role as giving him a *'helicopter view'* of the sector.

'*It helps*', he says, '*that today's young people are more community-minded than earlier generations.*' Purpose is important and, increasingly, it's the charity sector that responds first to disaster. When people leaving a concert at the Manchester Arena suffered a bomb attack, local Scouts raised more than £75,000 within 48 hours to support the victims. Few statutory agencies, Matt reminds us, can move that quickly.

Matt sees a very clear role for the charity sector in civil society, although he also sees the very real risk that government policy could change and marginalise those best able to meet need. There will always be a tension, he believes, between statutory agencies and the third sector.

Leadership style

As a leader, Matt sees himself as having an open style. He believes in transparency and personal authenticity. '*People have to want to do a good job, enjoy what they do and be recognised for the contribution they make,*' he tells me.

He also believes in letting his team see that he is not invincible. He's very open about the self-doubt he's experienced when forced to make tough decisions. He knows the importance of remaining objective and focused on doing the right thing, both for his family and the organisation he leads.

For Matt, the future is certain. He has no plans to move from the Scout Association. He gets a buzz out of seeing how his organisation changes lives. It's all about giving young people an opportunity to prove themselves and equip themselves for useful lives.

Key Points from Matt:
1. Never take continuing member support for granted. You have to constantly strive to improve both quality of service and value for money.
2. Meet CEOs of similar organisations to discuss common challenges and share good practice. You might have very different client groups, but encounter similar problems.
3. The third sector can often respond faster than the statutory sector to disasters. How equipped is your organisation?
4. If your organisation is facing inevitable change, it makes sense to be close to the debates that can influence your future.
5. Investing money in recruiting the best Trustees for your organisation is far better than relying on word of mouth.

Kuljit Sandhu,
Managing Director, RISE Mutual
www.risemutual.org @KuljitSandhu16

'We will only diversify to the level where our quality of service remains the same.'

Early sense of social justice
Growing up in Wolverhampton in the years immediately following Enoch Powell's 'rivers of blood' speech gave Kuljit Sandhu early exposure to prejudice and racism. It was a tense time and her family's strong Sikh faith encouraged her to look behind the taunts to try to understand why people were behaving as they were. She realised early in her life that fear and insecurity are often at the root of prejudice and hate.

A sense of social justice developed in Kuljit as she grew up. From the age of 18, she began volunteering with Victim Support. A sociology degree followed, then a Master's in criminology. She started working as a Probation Officer in Lambeth at the time of the 1995 Brixton riots which followed the death of a young black man in police custody.

In probation
Kuljit was on the career escalator in the Probation Service, rising quickly through management. But, in parallel, she came to recognise that, *'to change behaviour, you have to consider the wider family and community, not just the offender.'* This wasn't something that the Probation Service was particularly set-up to do.

This didn't stop Kuljit from trying. Within the confines of the public sector, innovation became a signature trait throughout Kuljit's career. She became particularly interested in domestic abuse, and equality issues. She developed group programmes aimed at breaking the offending cycle, recruiting those with lived experience to both the staff team and as volunteers.

Arise!
As funding became tighter as austerity started to bite, ten probation services, including London, were put out to tender under the government's Transforming Rehabilitation (TR) initiative. This allowed public service mutuals, owned by their employees to be formed.

Kuljit saw an opportunity. In 2013, she won Cabinet Office funding to explore spinning out the more innovative services she was leading out of the public sector as a subcontractor under Transforming Rehabilitation.

Taking mainly those probation services concerned with behaviour change and prevention of crime would make it easier to create a distinctive offer but also to find new purchasers beyond central government. All as part of an employee-owned business.

This was the transformation that Kuljit had in mind.

RISE MUTUAL CIC
- RISE – standing for Rehabilitation and Innovative Solutions Enterprise – has 160 staff, contracts with several London Borough Councils and a number of prisons in the Home Counties
- In its first year as a social enterprise, RISE dealt with more than 3,500 referrals from the criminal courts and case-managed more than 150 people subject to community orders
- Kuljit Sandhu became Managing Director upon launch of the public service mutual in 2015.

How to innovate

Following a long tendering process, in January 2015 RISE Mutual CIC was born, with Kuljit as its new managing director.

So, what happened? *'Independence has definitely made it easier to diversify, with RISE winning contracts with several councils very quickly after spinning out,'* she tells me.

However, Kuljit has been determined not to see the organisation lose its focus by taking on commissioned services that don't fit with the vision. The organisation's mission, she tells me, is clearly stated: *'to provide innovative solutions that transform lives – anything beyond that, isn't us.'*

Diversifying – opportunity and challenge
Morphing into an employee-owned mutual has made it easier for RISE to broaden its range of youth services. RISE now works with families affected by domestic abuse, troubled teenagers and their parents and youngsters who find school traumatic and fail to attend. But, as Kuljit explains: *'We will only diversify to the level where our quality of service remains the same – it is always better to do a few things well than many things badly.'*

Some of the top team in RISE adapted to independence better than others and there were a fair number of changes in the early months. There were people force-fit into jobs they couldn't do, in one case resulting in a serious operational crisis and a new appointment.

Also staff turnover is lower, she tells me, *'as people have come to appreciate the fact that they are the owners of the business.'* Employees are involved through a Staff Council attended by Kuljit and her senior team. One member of that Council also sits on the RISE Board of Directors.

Authentic leadership is effective leadership
Kuljit describes herself as 'authentic' in her leadership style. Accompanying her around her HQ, she knows everyone's names and seems to have time for people. She is supportive in outlook and yet people also know, when you ask them, what she stands for. It helps her, she says, that she has

'*strong personal values that resonate with the mission of the organisation I lead.*'

Shifting the culture

Moving forward a public-sector culture has been tough – and is a '*work-in-progress*'. In the traditional hierarchy of the probation service, it took time and effort to shift the culture from command and control to a more democratic, inclusive one. '*People get used to being told what to do and this isn't the way we want to operate in RISE,*' she tells me. When times have been tough, Kuljit, confesses, she has needed to be controlling, too. But, she tells me, '*I quickly revert to a more open and inclusive style when the crisis has passed – that I won't let go.*'

Unusually for a Chief Officer, Kuljit is also not afraid to step in to cover staff absence at the front line. She has been known to deliver an offender workshop with just five minutes' notice, rather than see it rescheduled. While conscious that this isn't 'normal', she wants to send a signal both that delivery always comes first and that, regardless of her current role, she is a probation professional just like her staff.

Reinforcing the brand

To make sure people felt they were part of something new, Kuljit ensured the organisation spent time on refreshing the brand. '*It's as important to remind our own people, as well as those who commission us, of where we are positioned in our marketplace, as a fresh, new approach to rehabilitation.*'

Here, winning awards definitely helps. Appropriately enough, RISE picked up the 'Rising Star' award of the Employee

Ownership Association, at the end of 2016. Something everyone takes pride in.

Building and balancing
Transformation for RISE has meant rapidly building new networks beyond the public sector. RISE now has strong links with academics and researchers in the field of criminal justice. Kuljit and her team have found themselves commissioned to deliver consultancy assignments for a range of UK and overseas organisations. RISE, Kuljit believes, will inevitably grow to work in other parts of the UK and abroad.

Through all this organisational transformation, family remains important to Kuljit. She lives outside London with her husband and two children. He is self-employed and works from home, which makes it easier for Kuljit to put in long hours when she has to. But equally, she makes sure she does not let work dominate her private life. Family time is how she finds the balance we all need.

Key Points from Kuljit:
1. **You need a clear vision of what you want to do when you take an organisation out of the public sector. It is too easy to follow the funding and lose sight of why you're there.**
2. **When you become a staff-owned mutual, you have to work on the culture, so that people feel listened to and able to play their part in decision making.**
3. **Whatever service you provide, you should aim to work with those who use your services, not do things for or to them.**
4. **Make sure you have your existing services delivered to the highest standard, and profitably, before taking on new things.**

5. Look at the emerging trends shaping societal behaviour and see how your organisation can evolve to meet tomorrow's need even more effectively than it can meet today's.

SECTION SIX

TURNAROUND LEADERSHIP

'Too many medium-sized charities have neither specialism nor scale. And, for many of them, merger or closer collaboration would make sense.'

Dan Corry, CEO, New Philanthropy Capital

Introduction

 From time to time, many social sector organisations find themselves in a mess. It may well be a financial crisis. Equally, it can be a situation where the organisation has become moribund.

Turnaround leadership differs from transformational leadership by its short-term nature and the fact that survival, not change, is often at stake.

So, what does turnaround leadership involve? Having been involved in several, I would say it has three elements. The first is the ability to see quickly what's going on, often with limited or poor management information. This involves both critical insight and, more importantly, a mindset that faces up to things.

The second is an ability to galvanise others around the 'burning platform' and get quick agreement to a plan. This means being able to convey to a variety of audiences that, if we don't act now, we are likely to fail. This sounds easy, but in the fraught context of mission-based organisations, this requires good emotional intelligence.

Turnaround normally involves action in a period of weeks that might otherwise take place over months, or even longer. This can involve dramatic changes in services, people and the cost base. Decisions in turnaround have to be drastic, often more than some stakeholders find it easy to understand.

The third ability of turnaround leaders is to see the plan through with resolve, without giving way on the substantive issues. Turnaround is very difficult medicine – but, if leaders can successfully administer it, then the door is open to the future.

The leadership of turnaround is quite different to everyday leadership, where consensus is normally the goal. It's more like being a surgeon than the conductor of an orchestra. It suits strong and decisive leaders. But, because it is so tough, the need to empathise is probably higher in turnaround situations than any other.

Turnaround leadership, in the social sector, is actually quite similar to turnaround in the business world. But there are two things that make it harder.

First, once there's a defensible plan, the re-financing of a business is often easier than in the social sector, where all changes have to be self-financing.

Second, the people side of turnaround is always harder, due to the distributed nature of power in social sector organisations and the fact that emotional issues tend to be greater.

Which makes these leaders all the more impressive.

The people we feature here are much more than turnaround leaders, but each has faced and succeeded in a turnaround scenario.

Kirsty McHugh didn't find a crisis when she arrived at the Employment and Related Services Association (ERSA), but an organisation that was moribund. She has since turned it into one of the most effective trade associations in the UK, with three quarters of its members from the third sector.

Rob Parkinson arrived at Home-Start UK in 2013, with the organisation in the doldrums. Since the departure of the founding CEO several years earlier, a string of CEOs had failed to arrest a decline in income and impact. Rob's response was to help the organisation understand its problems and institute a recovery plan involving the consolidation of 280 Home-Start schemes to probably around 60 by 2020.

Matt Stevenson Dodd of Street League walked into an organisation that had just lost its founder and was in a precarious position operationally and financially. He sorted that out and then made a huge challenge to his organisation to focus on its impact, leading to dramatic changes in its business model. Matt is now recognised nationally for his work in this area.

Kirsty McHugh, CEO, Employment Related Services Association
www.ersa.org.uk @ersa_news

'You've got to keep your eyes focused on what you want to achieve. You may need to think laterally. Your organisation may not survive. You may need to think about alliances, collaborations, adjacent markets.'

When Kirsty McHugh speaks, people listen. A decade or so ago, she took over as CEO of a sleepy trade-association for companies and charities in the 'welfare to work' business. Today, ERSA (the Employment Related Services Association) is a poster-child for how a trade body can punch well beyond its weight.

ERSA turnaround
When Kirsty arrived at ERSA it was *'with respect, slightly moribund, just me and a windowless office.'* She was, in her own words, *'very lucky – I had a great Board, some money in the bank and blank canvas.'* Kirsty got to work quickly

building a small but effective team, to build a successful subscription-based membership body.

The formula for this, she tells me is threefold:

'With membership organisations you need an offer, you need events – these are the heartbeat of a membership organisation. People join for the information – and the gossip – they want networks and to do business – and they want to feel they have some voice, advocacy. And you only retain members if you are good.'

But it hasn't all been plain-sailing with three changes of government, many ministerial and policy changes. There was a seesaw of political and financial interest in the employment sector. Much depended on the economy.

Further to this, devolution, austerity and the fragmentation of the employment sector have all meant ERSA has had to respond very quickly to remain relevant.

Resilience helps you as a leader in tough times
What is Kirsty's leadership style? In her own view, she prefers smaller organisations where the CEO can get things done. *'I am not big on processes, I am a goal-oriented person, I need good people around me.'*

What are Kirsty's achievements, aside from building ERSA? An important one, she says, has been changing the language from the American-style negative 'welfare to work' to the more positive term 'employment support'.

Her own philosophy, and that of ERSA, is that employment doesn't exist in a bubble and relates to a host of factors in the lives of people who might not be in work: their housing, their mental health, their family circumstances, the state of their community. The language of welfare to work doesn't reflect this and, partly thanks to ERSA, this is far less part of the discourse in this country.

The broader your range of key stakeholders the better
One of the distinctive features of ERSA is that it is cross-sector. Members range from large multi- sector outsourcers to small local charities. *'This is deliberately so,'* says Kirsty. While 80% of ERSA members are charities and social enterprises, many of them small, a handful of large companies in the association strengthen it, both in terms of credibility and influence.

How do the likes of G4S and the Salvation Army, both organisations with different ultimate focus, get along when put in the room together? *'Extremely well,'* says Kirsty. *'What people find is that they have a lot in common.'*

It is wrong, she tells me, to say that those leading business units within the private sector are any less committed to the people we are helping than someone working for a charity.

It just isn't like that in reality – *'there is good, bad and indifferent in all sectors and while commissioners sometimes say"we want a charity doing this", the truth of the matter is that often a private sector organisation will do the job just as well.'*

What does Kirsty do to keep body and soul together as a CEO? *'Time out to think,'* is her fast response. One of her things her staff like about her, she says, is her ability to work a way out of a difficult spot. This is only possible by taking some distance from the problem in hand. Not looking at work emails after early evening is an important discipline for Kirsty. And taking time out to go to the cinema (*'Monday is my cinema night'*) and theatre, often with her children, is vital to her sense of overall balance. She also tries to cut herself some slack: *'I am highly forgiving of myself,'* she says, just about keeping a straight face.

Humble beginnings

Unlike a lot of people in social leadership roles, who have been prepared for life at the top from a young age, this wasn't the case for Kirsty. Moving from East London to Huntingdon, a small town in Cambridgeshire, the eldest of four children, Kirsty's early life didn't prepare her for what was to come.

'I am the archetypal council house girl who did well at school, first to university, concerned about money. I came from a relatively affluent area – but we weren't.'

Like a lot of working class kids Kirsty had no big professional or family networks. As a consequence, when she left University College London with an English degree, she had no idea at all what to do next and retained that sense of *'no plan'* even though her career looks, at one level, a linear success.

She landed, after a while, at Business in the Community, where she spent ten years. She internalised Julia Cleverdon's well-known view that *'you can't change the world without balancing the books'*. Being on top of the money has always been a signature of Kirsty's approach.

Political animal

Business in the Community wasn't Kirsty's only job in her 20s and 30s. She combined this with a spell as a councillor in Lambeth where she held various portfolios, including the one for crime. She recalls her first meeting with the Chief Superintendent who asked a 26-year-old Kirsty, *'What's a nice girl like you doing in a place like this?'*

Rather than haughtily put the policeman right, Kirsty smiled, wisecracked and, over her tenure, built a productive relationship to get things done. Being a politician, Kirsty says, is a brilliant, often disregarded, preparation for being a CEO. *'As a councillor, you have to galvanise people, build coalitions, speak in public and get things done.'* She feels she couldn't have gone on to the roles she has without this vital preparation.

You can't map your future in advance, you have to be flexible and adapt to opportunity

What is her advice to her 25-year-old self? *'Don't try to map it all out in advance,'* is her message. *'Life is long, most of us will live longer, careers will need to be flexible, whilst retirement is often now a process. We all ought to be taking career breaks. Don't rush.'*

Kirsty learned about self-care the hard way. She went through a tough spell when working full-time for Business in the Community, being a Councillor with a portfolio, studying for her Masters and being a mother. As a result, she was so busy she didn't realise that she wasn't as happy as she needed to be. Time out from the day job during her second maternity leave gave Kirsty time to think and make decisions: she stepped down from the council and changed job. She hasn't looked back.

What drives Kirsty? Again, her answer is rapid: *'anger'*. Anger at the lack of opportunity afforded to so many people due to factors over which they had no control. She knows from her own life that opportunity is closed off to many people. Her own mother was denied the opportunity to take the 11 plus as her family couldn't afford the school uniform. Many of those she still knows have had lesser lives for lack of networks, confidence and opportunity.

This is what drives her on.

Tomorrow's leaders will need to be able to adapt quickly
So how does Kirsty think CEOs will succeed in the 2020s? Her view is that it's about adaptability and thinking deeply about the future and your place within it. *'You've got to keep your eyes focused on what you want to achieve. You may need to think laterally. Your organisation may not survive. You may need to think about alliances, collaborations, adjacent markets.'*

Her big message to today's CEOs and future leaders is this, *'You need time to think, to give yourself leave to think, whilst doing something else the cogs are often whirring in the background. It's about having other interests.'*

Key Points from Kirsty:
1. **Take time to think, take time off, have holidays and keep a range of interests.**
2. **Success over a career isn't necessarily about a linear path to the top, it's about taking time to do the thing you really want and need in life – because work is only a part of life.**
3. **The third sector hasn't got a monopoly on being caring or successful in the social sector – and it's often unhelpful to caricature the private sector in a negative way.**

4. The future is going to be won by CEOs who are lateral thinkers, alliance-builders: people who can respond imaginatively to the challenging economic and political environment.
5. Politics, whether local or national, can be an excellent apprenticeship for successful CEOs in our sector.

Rob Parkinson, CEO, Home-Start UK
www.home-start.org.uk
Parkinson @CEOhomestart

'It can be tempting to chase the money, but it's always best to stick to what you do best, and not be led away from why your organisation exists.'

It begins with music

Rob Parkinson was born in 1973 – at around the time Home-Start was founded by Margaret Harrison in his home city of Leicester. By coincidence, Rob's parents knew Margaret. His father was running the local CVS at the time and helped Margaret write her first funding bid.

Margaret did not set out to create a global federated charity, although that is what grew over the ensuing 40 years. There are now Home-Start charities in almost every corner of the UK and in more than 20 countries worldwide.

Similarly, Rob did not set out to be a charity CEO. He grew up with a passion for music and trained as both a singer and pianist. But it was perhaps inevitable that growing up in a home where community volunteering was the norm, that he would follow a career in the charity sector.

After a degree in politics, Rob's first job was in dementia care with Methodist Homes for the Aged; a Christian charity that focused on care. He stayed there for five years before joining The National Deaf Children's Society. He returned to Leicester as CEO of a charity that provides accommodation and support to people who find themselves homeless.

HOME-START
- Home-Start supports families by matching them with volunteers, who help the parents of young children through the barriers that life too often puts in the way
- A network of more than 300 member Home Start charities supplies 15,000 home visiting volunteers supporting 30,000 families at any one time
- CEO since 2013, Rob Parkinson is leading the transformation of this large charity brand.

Becoming inspired

It was working with homeless people that inspired Rob to apply when Home-Start was seeking a new CEO in 2008.

'Too many of the people I was working with were saying how they wished more had been done for them when they were children, and in Home-Start, I could see an opportunity that provided that much needed early support.'

Home-Start was not having an easy time when Rob joined as CEO. The national organisation had been running at a loss and had seen some dramatic cost-cutting as it fought to survive. It was not easy to manage a network of more than 300 local Home-Start charities. Rob quickly learned that running a federation was very different from other charity structures.

The organisation had also been wrestling with a reduction in the funding generally available for family support. The universality of Home-Start support (there is no means-test) doesn't always sit comfortably with public sector commissioners, who often prefer to fund targeted interventions that conquer specific problems.

Yet, if you talk to any of the 15,000 home visiting volunteers around the Home-Start network you soon see that it is often the simple act of befriending that makes the difference. Home-Start is all about early intervention, nipping in the bud things that could so easily escalate if not promptly addressed. While early intervention is often talked about as a solution, funding has, sadly, run in the opposite direction in recent years.

Turning around a federation
Running a federation is quite different to running a large organisation. Rob's office has a team of just 35 people, supporting a network of more than 300 member charities which together employ thousands of people.

Communication is clearly important and Rob works hard at being visible and accessible to his members.

'You have to give a vast amount of yourself to a job like this,' he explains, adding, *'We don't have all the answers at the*

centre,' he said, *'but can usually introduce someone with recent relevant experience.'*

I note Rob's point that running a federation should be a step on the career journey of any leader with national ambition.

Turnaround by consolidation

Local Home-Start charities are not immune from the ever-larger contracts that are becoming increasingly common across the sector. Commissioners, Rob tells me, *'are increasingly wanting to award a single contract over a Local Authority area. This is encouraging local Home-Starts to merge to form single county or even sub-regional organisations.'*

Inevitably, mergers can create tensions, with not everyone seeing the benefit. It's quite clear to me that much of Rob's time is taken up managing what is an inevitable change from units of organisation that are super-local (with all this brings, good and bad) to larger units more able to compete for available funding.

It would be easy to get frustrated by those unable or unwilling to see this bigger picture. This perhaps is where leadership becomes important. Rob is not someone to lose his cool. Or take a short-term win over a long-term result. Leadership in a federation is not about imposing your will onto the members.

Instead, Rob talks of having to cajole and gently persuade, as well as inspiring through patient exposition of what is working well up and down the country. Rob's role as turnaround leader could be likened to that of an impresario, setting the stage upon which his members can perform well.

Getting the balance right

Rob reads widely, but doesn't claim to follow any one particular leadership style. He describes how he *'intuitively hoovers up ideas he can use'* from those he meets, hears or reads about.

The days of a CEO always being in the office with no home life are long gone. Rob is keen that people appreciate and value the fact that we can all be more effective if we have a good work life balance. Rob is a keen sportsman and cricketer. He's a Leicester City season ticket holder and is also a keen runner.

As a boy, Rob's ambition was to be a professional musician. He has kept that interest alive and can often be found at his piano (he has a white one!). Is making music from a large number of different notes and chords a metaphor for turning around a troubled federation?

True or not, at Home-Start Rob seems to be playing the right tune.

Key Points from Rob:
1. **All organisations have to evolve over time and some will inevitably find this difficult.**
2. **Leading a federation requires different skills to running a large, single organisation.**
3. **A focus on behaviour and relationships is absolutely central to organisational success.**
4. **It's important to focus on what you do well, not what pays best.**
5. **A good work life balance is important not just for you, but for your team.**

Matt Stevenson-Dodd, CEO, Street League
www.streetleague.co.uk @Matt_SD

Baptism of fire

In 2010, Street League was advertising for a new CEO. It was in trouble following the messy departure of its founder. One of its funders was keeping the lights on. So as an applicant, Matt knew he would have his work cut out from the off.

Matt found the organisation's use of football to teach young people new skills and help them find jobs appealing. He was successful and took the helm.

STREET LEAGUE

- UK Street League is a sport for employment charity, founded in 2003, whose purpose today is to bring an end to youth unemployment in the UK, currently at 1 in 7 people aged 16–24
- Operating in 14 regions across the UK, Street League's sport for employment programmes run in 36 local communities
- Becoming CEO in 2010, Matt Stevenson-Dodd has effectively turned a grant-reliant charity into an effective business.

Transforming the model

Experience as a CEO told Matt that Street League would do better if it focused more on what it did best. He wanted to move from counting numbers of people showing up to counting real outcomes. Football became the focus and helping 16–25-year-olds find jobs the target.

Street League had been founded a few years earlier by a well-intentioned young doctor. It was his response to seeing the same faces appearing time again at A & E. The charity created a football league formed of homelessness projects. As it evolved over time, so it diversified into other sports, diluting its brand. Matt decided, very quickly, to bring it back to what it did best.

Transforming the money

When Matt took over, Street League was reliant on grants, with 90% of its income secured from successful bids. Today, about of half Street League's income comes from corporate sponsorship. Grant income now represents just 10% of the total. Public contracts make up the rest. In many ways, he says, Street League is now a business, delivering value to customers.

The power of focus
Matt knows the importance of focus. At times, he has refused funding when attached to outcomes he does not view as core to Street League's offer. Dilution is no good, he says. Matt believes that, in time, funders will respect this clarity and be more likely to offer their support. To back this up, he tells me of at least one grant-maker that has adapted its funding criteria to enable them to contribute to Street League's continuing success.

Celebrating failure as well as success
In a world where everyone is quick to shout about their achievements, it's refreshing to read in Street League's annual report about its failures. A headline in the charity's 2015/6 annual report reads: '*Last year, we weren't able to help 109 young people.*'

This is then qualified, explaining that these were among 1,685 young people who started the Street League programme. Too few admit that they simply cannot help everyone. '*It's the learning from those that fall through the net that strengthens the services offered to those that succeed,*' Matt argues.

Matt has been personally associated with a drive in the sector to develop a more honest and transparent narrative about success. This highlights the fact that charities should take risks by engaging a wider range of people, and, as a result, won't always be successful.

Harvard learning-lens

In 2012, Matt won a scholarship to attend a strategic course on non-profit management at Harvard Business School. This encouraged him to see his organisation through a different lens. As a result, he's explored social franchising as a different way to scale up the work of the organisation.

Transforming the Board

Matt has also been ambitious when seeking out new Trustees. As Chair of Street League, Mike Parker used to head up Dow Chemicals and British Nuclear Fuels and brings a global perspective to the organisation. Other Street League Trustees are also high fliers in their chosen careers. A Board of high achieving Trustees can only raise the level of what is expected from the organisation, Matt believes.

Early learning

How did Matt turn out as he has? Growing up in a Nottinghamshire mining village gave Matt Stevenson-Dodd early exposure to social inequality. The 1984 miners' strike split the small community. Matt's adoptive father was not a miner, so he did not experience the same hardships as many of his schoolmates. But the clashes between flying pickets and police officers left their mark. Matt was only 11 years old.

Later, Matt volunteered at a local youth club, took a gap year in South America, then studied Community and Youth Work at Plymouth University.

Learning another way

Joining Nottinghamshire County Council as a youth worker, Matt felt *'it was rather like learning to drive, with the real learning only starting when I qualified and was out in the field.'*

He attributes much of that learning to Anne, an experienced youth worker who was his mentor in those early years.

Matt left the Council to set up Unique, a café-based youth project in Newark, Notts. Support for youngsters excluded from school was evolving and Matt developed alternative education courses, delivered by Unique. This won the support of funders and service users alike. Cheaper than many alternatives and more effective, everybody benefited.

Help change more young lives
Matt recognised that many youngsters were 'activist pragmatists', whereas the education system favoured 'theorist reflectors'. To put it simply, they want to learn by doing, rather than by listening to a teacher and learning in an organised, tidy way.

As Unique grew, so too did Matt's determination to grow the organisation. A friend was doing an MBA and, after talking with him, Matt enrolled with Nottingham University Business School to do the same. Most of his group were from the private sector, so there was lively debate as he sought to translate shareholder return into stakeholder value.

Fifteen years later, as CEO of charity Street League, Matt is funding two of his senior managers through MBA programmes. I can see how he recognises the importance of measuring social impact in terms funders will understand.

Evolving
As a leader, Matt says his style has evolved over the years. He sees himself as tough when he must be, but always very approachable.

He knows the value of listening to people, be they corporate sponsors, staff members or service users. His team is now empowered to run the operation, with his role as CEO increasingly about building the relationships for tomorrow's success.

Throughout his career Matt has benefited from having a mentor; someone with the experience and wisdom to *'help me see the wood for the trees, with whom I can share my concerns.'* Today, he mentors other emerging CEOs, helping them grow their organisations and careers.

Living differently
When Matt took the Young Enterprise job, he moved to north Wales, where his wife grew up and her parents live. He still lives there today, spending three days a week in London and two working from home. This forces him to be strict about how he spends his time. Meetings are usually held on London days and he catches up on office work in north Wales.

A benefit of living in north Wales is that he can soon lose himself in the hills on his mountain bike. It's where he does his best thinking. He also plays bass guitar in a band and once, many years ago, almost won a record deal.

Life for Matt could so easily have taken a completely different course!

Key Points from Matt
1. **Be honest and transparent about what your organisation does well, but also what it doesn't do well. Much can be learned from making mistakes.**

2. Anyone can tick boxes. Focus on making and measuring real social impact, using terms your funders will understand.

3. Delivering real value to corporate sponsors can deliver far greater security of income than chasing grants or public-sector contracts.

4. Never sit on your laurels and think you've arrived. There's always something new to learn and new ways to help your organisation evolve.

5. Making time to be outside, close to nature, can stimulate your creativity as well as keep you fit. We all need to lead a balanced life.

SECTION SEVEN

CHARISMATIC LEADERSHIP

'If you're contemplating leading a spin-out, first think smartly about what you are trying to do and why. Second, make sure you bring your team with you. Without their wholehearted support, you will really struggle.'

Alison Reid, CEO, Community Dental Services

Introduction

In a *Psychology Today* article, Dr Ron Riggio defined charismatic leaders as 'essentially very skilled communicators, individuals who are both verbally eloquent but also able to communicate to followers on a deep emotional level.'

The social sector abounds with charismatic leaders. Often founders, these leaders are passionate individuals who others are drawn towards. Their personal vision has a great deal of influence over how the organisation is run.

The upsides are that these leaders attract resources, attention and talent into an organisation. Charismatic leaders galvanise. At best, they embody the essence of what leadership is taken to mean.

The downsides are that the charismatic leader is often not a detail person, that organisations can become dependent on them and that, as people of feeling, they can often be difficult to persuade. Their organisations are prone to getting stuck.

Sat Singh founded the Renaissance Foundation as a teenager. He is a person of incredible energy, enlisting the support of luminaries such as Barack Obama to his cause. But, as he tells us, he has found the business of running an organisation very challenging.

Dawn Hewitt became CEO of the two merged organisations in 2000, took CHUMS from the NHS into social enterprise in 2011, and today continues to create clinically based services for children, young people and their families across Luton, Bedfordshire and beyond. Dawn is a standout person with a true gift for bringing people on-side, whether these are commissioners or families.

Kevin Davis, while not a founder, has, for 20 years, been the driving force of The Vine Trust in the West Midlands. I first met Kevin at a pitch meeting several years ago where he turned up bearing gold bars to represent the 'Goldmine' he would create through the investment. He got the money and won our hearts too. Kevin runs on passion and, as a Christian, faith too. We explore how this all works for him.

Sat Singh, CEO, Renaissance Foundation
www.renaissance-foundation.com
@RF_Tweets

'Things eventually happen if you follow your inspiration. This gets you through the very dark days, when success feels a long way off.'

Yes, you can
You get sick at the age of 14 and are told you have a life-limiting condition. You fall behind at school, are dyslexic and get in with the wrong crowd. And you are affected by close family members with alcohol problems.

For many people, the life that followed would be one of predictable under-achievement and worse. For Sat Singh, this same life became the personal motive force behind the charity Renaissance Foundation, which he set up at the age of 18 in a McDonald's in East London using one 'pay as you go' mobile phone.

RENAISSANCE FOUNDATION

- Based in East London, Renaissance Foundation is a community-based educational charity, working with young people aged 13–19 living with major challenges, at risk of failing to achieve their potential
- Specifically, Renaissance works with transitioning hospital patients, young carers and school pupils at risk
- Having set up Renaissance at the age of 18, Sat Singh is Chief Exec of a thriving charity that has just celebrated its 10th birthday.

Inspirational ways forward

The idea of Renaissance Foundation was very simple: provide an inspirational way out for young people living with significant life challenges. So, Sat set up programmes in East London for young carers, young hospital patients and young people at risk of falling into gangs.

Renaissance Foundation's young people attend long-term programmes which build towards an encounter with a key role model or leader. In 2016, Renaissance Foundation students met and interviewed Formula One driver Lewis Hamilton. In 2014, they attended the Nobel Peace Prize in Oslo, where they had down-time with Malala, the young Afghan activist for girls' and women's rights across the world.

Access to heroes

One of Sat's many jobs – in what is still a small team – is to help young people to kick down the doors they need to gain access to the top-level people they want to meet.

In this, Sat has a unique, understated skill. '*I just ask people,*' he tells me, hesitantly. What Sat has, that he doesn't fully understand, are the kind of alpha-networking skills that only the lucky few possess. The list of people he has persuaded to meet Renaissance Foundation's young members is rather impressive and includes (yes) President Obama while on his UK visit ('*They couldn't tell us we were meeting him*').

An early motivator for Sat was a chance meeting with Richard Williams, father of Venus and Serena, while at Wimbledon in his late teens (again, networks!). The Williams sisters came from the hardscrabble district of Compton, LA. But, with father Richard as their coach, both came to dominate women's tennis.

Richard Williams told Sat that he needed 'to see people as the same as himself, not above or below'. This advice stuck with him, as he tried to get his own organisation off the ground.

Feast and famine
The early years of Renaissance Foundation were, relatively speaking, quite bountiful. This was the New Labour era; the money was flowing and a twenty-something social entrepreneur with a compelling back-story was always going to find support.

Then, in 2010, the money stopped and Sat spent the next three years fighting 'hand to mouth' to keep the organisation afloat. Like many organisations, Renaissance Foundation had taken large government contracts and used this to grow a staff team and fund a proper HQ. But, with austerity, all this had to be wound down very quickly, an experience Sat found '*pretty traumatising.*'

Yet Sat learned a vital lesson. Impact for Renaissance Foundation wasn't going to happen through scale. Innovation was the key – then spreading the word. *'Growing the turnover and headcount actually had a bad effect on the creativity and identity of Renaissance Foundation during those years,'* he tells me. All his own effort went into managing staff and the operations. The activities and programmes of Renaissance Foundation ended up being increasingly funder-driven.

Impact matters
The impact you have is more important than the size of your organisation. As he manoeuvred Renaissance Foundation through near-death during those three difficult years from 2010, Sat resolved that he would make an impact by example. He would keep things small, tight and use the power of digital communication to spread the message of Renaissance Foundation more widely.

Yes, he would grow, not least to create the solid management team to free him to play his 'A Game' of networking and next-hill adventuring. But, the seven-digit turnover isn't something that lights his fire today.

Like many social entrepreneurs, Sat has shown incredible staying-power, often without a salary. Such self-sacrifice is, he knows, not sustainable as he hits his thirties and looks towards settling down and laying the ground for succession.

A big challenge will be to move Renaissance Foundation to a more solid financial footing. His *'exit strategy,'* as he calls it, will be to become an 'Ambassador' for Renaissance Foundation, probably operating from the Board, with a

Managing Director in place. He hopes to achieve this by 2022, when he will be 35 and Renaissance Foundation will be in its 18th year of operation.

Ideas attract

In common with the majority of social entrepreneurs, Sat's greatest strengths are his fervour for new ideas and magnetic energy. Both draws people in and they stay alongside him, often for many years.

His weaknesses are a lack of appetite for management, a discomfort with administrative detail and tendency to plough on without looking up often enough. To remedy this, Sat is looking to do an advanced social business programme at one of the big American universities, in one of the coming years.

Sat has no regrets whatsoever about the course he has taken, even though he is aware that he could have done very well in a commercial business.

Money has no intrinsic interest to Sat. Which is probably why he hasn't raised as much for Renaissance Foundation as someone with his communication gifts might have. This led him to seek out an audience for Renaissance Foundation members with Richard Branson, who, after many months, invited a group to visit him at his Oxfordshire home.

Life has a habit of putting obstacles in your way

Sat puts his distinctive outlook down to his early brush with mortality at the age of 14. Diagnosed with a serious immune-deficiency disorder, he was in and out of hospital for two years, missing a lot of school. Some of the treatments Sat was given had serious side effects. He was prepared for the possibility that his life might be considerably shortened by his illness.

While he eventually made a full recovery, Sat felt that the urgency this episode instilled in him put him in a hurry to make the most of every year of his life, to not waste time. *'My restlessness,'* he says, *'dates from that time,'*

Next
The day after we meet, Sat is going to meet a local NHS trust to promote Renaissance Foundation's programme for young patients, one of whom he is supporting to become a designer, following a heart-transplant at the age of 13. *'For many of these young people, life looks like it would be short. Getting it back isn't straightforward, there has been a lot of confidence, education and networks lost. We help put that back.'*

In the afternoon, he's going to see a famous football chairman who will hold a dinner in support of Renaissance Foundation next year.

We can learn a lot from Sat Singh. Many people in our sector get labelled as 'exceptional', 'talented' or 'unusual'. In reality, relatively few people truly deserve these accolades. They are often simply very good at what they do and have benefited from a lifetime of support to get there.

Sat took a very unpromising beginning and turned his own negative experience into an organisation that has enriched the lives of young people experiencing similar difficulties to his own. To do this without the head-start most of us in this sector receive is nothing short of extraordinary.

Key Points from Sat:

1. You can see your own life experiences as a starting point for social activism.
2. Like many social entrepreneurs, you may have core skills of passion and magnetic energy – and weaknesses around organisational development and management.
3. Ways to create social impact can vary – sometimes it's around scaling. At other times it's about creating innovative models or spreading the word about them through digital media.
4. The 'exit strategy' for a social entrepreneur needs early consideration if the venture is to be sustainable.
5. Mentors and inspiring figures can be huge factors in a social entrepreneur's life.

Dawn Hewitt, CEO, CHUMS
www.chums.uk.com @CHUMSCharity

'Growing a new business, even one spun out as an existing operation, is like raising a child. You have to nurture it, help it develop and then support it to become independent, with a mind of its own.'

Finding true vocation

It was a serious car accident that changed the course of Dawn Hewitt's career. She'd trained to become a district nursing sister. Her interest in palliative care was leading her towards becoming a Macmillan Nurse. With a back injury making lifting difficult, she started volunteering at a local hospice, as part of her recovery.

As one thing led to another, Dawn found herself managing a small child bereavement organisation called CHUMS, then part of the NHS. She had a part-time assistant and a team of 10 bereavement volunteers. Her time volunteering at the hospice had introduced her to the difficulties children can

162

face adjusting to life following the death of someone special. Dawn had found her true vocation.

Founding a charity

Dawn developed some creative ways to support bereaved children and referral numbers grew. Her growing team worked with whole families, not just the child. The results were heartening. But Dawn knew there was more that could be done. So, in 2007 she founded a charity, Friends of CHUMS.

Children deal with bereavement in different ways. Following a suicide or homicide, some display symptoms of post-traumatic stress disorder. The charity funded support for these children. The CHUMS charity now also funds a specialist suicide bereavement service, partnering with Bedfordshire police to provide valuable early trauma support, as well as several other early intervention services.

Adding strategic skills

As the team continued to grow, Dawn signed up for a Master's degree in Clinical/Organisational Leadership. This helped her develop the strategic skills she needed as the CHUMS service grew. It was a great foundation for what was to follow a few years later.

Still part of the NHS, the organisation became more and more autonomous. When the 'Right to Request' programme came along, it seemed the obvious way to guarantee the long-term future of the CHUMS service. Child bereavement support was already delivered by charities rather than the NHS in other parts of the UK. Social enterprise was the obvious way to go and CHUMS social enterprise CIC was born in June 2011.

CHUMS CIC
- CHUMS started in 1997 as two voluntary child bereavement organisations in the north and south of Bedfordshire and, by 2000, was receiving 40 bereavement referrals and had 16 volunteers
- CHUMS now receives around 3,100 referrals per year and has 59 staff as well as 120+ volunteers supporting a number of services
- Dawn Hewitt became CEO of the two merged organisations in 2000, took CHUMS from the NHS into social enterprise by 2011, and today continues to create clinically based services for children, young people and their families across Luton, Bedfordshire and beyond.

Shock of the new

The new venture got off to a flying start, securing a contract to deliver Tier 2 CAMHS services in Bedfordshire, in addition to child bereavement support.

'It was both exciting and terrifying,' Dawn admits. *'I had no experience of running a company and here I was with a new and already diversifying social enterprise.'*

The new contract doubled the size of CHUMS overnight and Dawn found herself inevitably further from the coalface. Missing the service user contact, she recognised that, to grow the organisation to support more young people, her future lay in the office.

A good way to grow is to provide more services for the same client group. Six years on, bereavement support remains an important part of what CHUMS does, but its services are now far wider. There is a focus on early intervention and prevention across all nine clinical services. CHUMS has developed some innovative and creative ways of delivering services that break down the stigma surrounding mental health, using football, music and film making.

Growing pains and gains

Over the past 20 years, Dawn has grown CHUMS from a very small team within the NHS to a thriving, vibrant social enterprise. She has no plans to move on to another challenge. She still enjoys what she does at CHUMS far too much to ever consider leaving.

The journey has not been without its bumps. Rapid growth can bring with it cash flow problems and Dawn admits they had something of a crisis in their third year of trading. Due to Dawn's tenacity and determination to succeed, CHUMS secured several new contracts in a few months and had an external investor on standby to loan them the cash if they needed it. Changes were made to the finance function to make sure better management information was always at Dawn's fingertips.

Having a charity alongside the social enterprise opens new doors. Just as CHUMS has flourished since spinning out of the NHS, so too has its charity wing grown. Last year, 20% of CHUMS' income came from the charity. As well as fundraising, the charity also has an important role spreading the word about the work CHUMS does. Sometimes it's easier for someone else to sing your praises than to sing your own.

Listening to service users
The service user perspective is always present at CHUMS.

'Connect' is an award-winning service user participation group that meets weekly to help CHUMS focus on what is important.

Service users assist in so many ways – from sitting on interview panels, to speaking at conferences and writing literature. The Board takes the service user perspective very seriously. It keeps the organisation grounded in the realities of its work.

Measuring impact
Measuring impact is an important part of each child's journey with CHUMS.

Dawn's team rigorously monitor outcomes to ensure they make the difference that children and young people deserve. *'Having a good bank of impact data really helps us when bidding for new work,'* Dawn explains.

CHUMS is now funded by a number of NHS Trusts, schools and other commissioners. It also helps that CHUMS has started to pick up awards, recently collecting a Queen's Award for Volunteering.

The boss, the team and the Board
Dawn entered the nursing profession because she wanted to change lives. Inspired as a girl by Florence Nightingale, Dawn says she's inspired every day by the kindness and creativity shown by her team. She knows, that if she was no longer there, the organisation would continue to evolve

without her support. *'It's good to know I'm not indispensable,'* she adds.

The CHUMS team is also a small team, certainly compared to others described in this book. Dawn describes her leadership style as *'friendly but firm.'* She knows that lines have to be drawn and that when push comes to shove, she is the boss.

In this, Dawn is supported by a small Board. One member is an accountant, another a GP. One is a strategist and the Chair is a businessman and parent whose family were supported when their son died.

Remembering to look after ourselves
Working with children, particularly those affected by bereavement, can take its toll on your own mental health. *'It's important to have empathy,'* says Dawn, *'but equally, you know you can't bring mummy back, however much the child would like that to happen.'*

In an organisation such as CHUMS, it's important that every member of the team feels supported. New joiners go through a rigorous induction process, which includes time with Dawn. Company culture is tolerant of mistakes, accepting that in a person-centred service it is impossible to get things right all the time. So much of the learning in this job is on the job, rather than in a classroom.

Working at CHUMS offers a range of opportunities to work on your own wellbeing. From lunchtime walks in surrounding parkland to a personal fitness trainer and advice on diet and healthy eating.

Belonging
value.

Dawn knows that looking after herself is as important as looking after the team. *'If I'm OK, then there's more chance the team will also be OK,'* she says. She makes sure she makes time for family and friends and enjoys theatre and walking with her dog.

Key Points from Dawn:
1. **Diversification is good. It can be easier if the client group remains the same. There's a lot to learn if you are going to deliver new things to an audience with whom you're not familiar.**
2. **Growing a business is like raising a child. One day it will no longer need you; that's success.**
3. **Service user participation can help keep the debate aligned with reality.**
4. **Setting up a charity to run alongside your social enterprise can give you greater funding freedom and make innovation easier to afford.**
5. **Look after yourself and it will be easier to look after others.**

Kevin Davis, CEO, The Vine Trust
www.vinetrustgroup.co.uk @KevinRDavis

'In an increasingly confused world, people prefer to work with organisations with a clear, understandable set of values.'

Evangelical inspiration
Like it or not, some of the world's most successful charities have their roots in religion. Some go back centuries, with their histories intertwined with that of the organised church. Others are more recent, inspired by a new generation of vibrant, evangelical groups.

Kevin Davis has just completed twenty years as CEO of Walsall-based charity the Vine Trust Group. He grew up in a family with strong Christian faith. Before he graduated with a degree in Government and Management, he started volunteering with the then recently formed Vine Trust.

169

THE VINE TRUST
- With foundations set firmly within the Christian faith, the Vine Trust Group is a Community Development Trust supporting young people aged 13–25 for whom the system has failed
- Based in Walsall, West Midlands, the organisation runs a mix of services and facilities, focused on 'hard to reach' young people not attending school and at risk of falling into crime and drugs
- Having volunteered at the charity since 1997, Kevin Davis was invited by the Trustees in 2010 to become CEO at just 36 years old, marking the event by crowdfunding £50,000.

Foundations

The Vine Trust charity had been set up by a group of local churches united in their vision to do more to support 'at risk' young people. Kevin volunteered at the charity's then base, a former rough pub, 'The Vine', that had been converted into a youth venue.

With the charity's non-judgemental approach, the former pub became a popular venue. *'It was OK to just come in, drink a glass of pop and play a game of pool,'* Kevin explains. He's also quick to point out that sharing the Christian faith is about deeds, as well as words. And that finding that balance was a challenge for the early pioneers.

Early responsibility

When the CEO moved on, the Trustees invited Kevin to step in as interim CE. Just 23 years old, Kevin was pursuing a commercial career, but accepted the challenge.

He has benefited from the support of a Board who are all committed to the vision and mission of the organisation. There is a shared belief that, if they set out to do the right things, they will get the right results. Unlike many charities, the Vine Trust don't sit on large reserves, but choose instead to put as much as they can spare into front line services.

Beyond charitable activity there is as an innovative group of social enterprises. The Vine Trust Group has a diverse range of income streams – from trading income to public sector grants – and has also had the courage to successfully seek social investment to fund new ventures.

Growing with the organisation
Kevin's job has grown as the organisation has grown and diversified over the years into Education, Employment, and Enterprise. The charity now turns over more than £3m a year. In 2017, through forming the Mercian Trust – a subsidiary, multi-academy trust – it will see substantial growth.

As a Community Development Trust, the organisation has evolved under Kevin's stewardship to provide a wide range of work, live, play, learn and worship activities to support wider communities and young people aged between 13 and 25. The philosophy has been the 'economy of together', creating a network of interlinked ventures, united in a common purpose, that interact with cross-sector stakeholders, looking for the 'win-win'.

In its educational work, the Vine Trust started out running pupil referral units. Now, with the advent of the Mercian Trust, it has six secondary schools under its wing – a mix of alternative provision, grammar, comprehensive and vocational schools.

Young people who come to the Vine Trust have often dropped out of mainstream schooling, so the education offer includes an innovative Studio School, focused on vocational, rather than academic pathways.

Over the past few years, the numbers of young people able to find employment within the group has increased. Kevin talks of youngsters who have made the full journey from disaffected youth to qualified and employed adult, all under the umbrella of the Vine Trust.

Transition is the challenge

For troubled young people, the transition from school to college or work can be particularly challenging. Kevin and his team became increasingly involved in helping young people secure work.

As a result, a number of Vine's social enterprises now provide opportunities for employment and apprenticeships. Activities include grounds maintenance and experience in furniture retail and a growing number of Vine restaurants. The restaurant trade is not easy and gives Kevin a few headaches. But, of all the social enterprises, the restaurants provide the greatest opportunity for young people to impress the wider public.

Over the past 20 years, the numbers have grown significantly. Leading royal and media-backed 'Ladder' Apprenticeship campaigns have secured over 3,000 apprenticeships. Forming the multi-academy trust means being responsible for more than 5,000 young people and 500 staff.

It recalls where the organisation started, providing welcoming entry points to the Vine family of ventures. In fact, the former Vine pub remains at the heart of the organisation, with more than 300 young people receiving coaching there, as well as having a good time.

Always values-led
An unashamedly Christian organisation, the Vine Trust does find this stance subject to probing from time to time. The humanist movement in Britain expressed public concern about a faith-led organisation running a Studio School. Kevin is quick to point out that Vine's schools are not faith schools, just schools run by some great people of faith, whose 'life sails' are filled by their spiritual convictions.

That said, just as many Catholic or Church of England schools are oversubscribed due to their focus on values. Those in the Vine Trust Group are popular with students and staff alike.

Time to study
After many years leading a successful organisation through the turbulence of growth, many CEOs would be content to sit back and enjoy what they have achieved. Kevin, however, accepted an invitation from Aston University to study for an MBA in 2015.

Kevin found the challenge of balancing his usual intuitive approach with the rigour of an academic framework stimulating. His organisation has inevitably benefited from his return to study. *'It's also introduced me to a whole new network of contacts, which creates further opportunities for collaboration and joint ventures.'*

As part of his MBA, Kevin and his senior team went through a 360 degree appraisal process. Not surprisingly, Kevin scored highly on relationships and was considered by his team to be a transformational leader. *'This business is all about people, so I was not surprised to have this confirmed as how the staff view me.'*

Time to reflect
Kevin's advice to anyone who finds themselves leading a third sector organisation is to be tenacious, patient and never give up.

He also values good listening and taking time to reflect on challenges, rather than rush at them unprepared.

Kevin knows where he's leading his organisation and why. He's mindful of the need to take his people with him. *'As with life itself, leading a team is to take them on a journey. It has to be a journey they're happy to take and lead to goals they want to reach as much as you do.'*

Key Points from Kevin:
1. **Faith inspired mission is more than just church services.**
2. **As your organisation grows, new opportunities will emerge, but never lose sight of your core mission and the work that has got you to where you are today.**
3. **Creating spaces where young people can work, live, play, learn and worship, would be on everyone's agenda, irrespective of faith, or no faith.**

4. Never stop learning; you're never too old to gain a new qualification.
5. Overcomers overcome! However tough the going gets, if you're 100% sure you're right, hang in and keep pushing. It's surprising how many people give up just before the victory they deny themselves.

SECTION EIGHT

FUNDER LEADERSHIP

'Social investment is neither a silver bullet nor applicable for all charities. It should be seen as part of the toolkit that a Finance Director has at their disposal to create impact.'

Mark Salway, Cass Business School

Introduction

Funding is the one thing that even the most rational CEO occasionally loses sleep over. It tops the polls every time.

Historically, grant funding in the UK tended, even in the good times, to be conservative and risk-averse. Grants were scattered in an uncoordinated way among thousands of organisations, often for small, time-limited projects of hugely varying quality.

When the music stopped in 2010 - and money became scarcer - this approach was exposed as unfit for purpose. There was a call for funders to be more discriminating, to look more closely at impact and to work together more as 'co-investors'. Interest also grew in new types of finance, including loans and outcome-related funding.

Around that time, innovation started to occur among the more progressive grant funders. Which is why we feature **Nat Sloane** who, as chair of the Big Lottery in England, has moved that organisation towards a longer-term view of funding and a more selective approach to funding, based on who is doing the most innovative and influential work.

Likewise, **Andy Ratcliffe**, of strategic grant-maker, Impetus-PEF, is using that organisation's money as 'leverage' to multiply many times over the resources (donations, in-kind support, public money) available to the organisations Impetus is working with.

Loans have taken a more prominent role in the funding landscape. It was in response to this that **Ben Rick** set up Social and Sustainable Capital. Giving up a successful City career, Ben has risked his own money, time and reputation to set up what is now one of the biggest of the UK's social finance intermediaries, which manages a fund of £50m.

How social impact is to be financed in the UK long-term is still not clear. Many believed that social finance would by now be playing a bigger role than it is. Others felt that it is only ever likely to be a bit-part player.

What cannot be denied now is that those who fund the social sector are working together as never before to create leverage and to be more discriminating in their approach, based on which organisations are having impact.

Nat Sloane, Chair,
Big Lottery Fund England,
www.biglotteryfund.org.uk/england
@BigLotteryFund

'You have to be bloody resilient! There is no financial upside in the social sector – there has to be long-term motivation beyond the self.'

Founder Mentor

When I am asked about the one person who has influenced my adult life the most, my answer is always 'Nat Sloane'.

We sit down at the organisation where we first met, 15 years ago – the charity Impetus-PEF – when Nat was a recent founder and I an ambitious young social entrepreneur.

Back then, Impetus-PEF was just Nat and his co-founder Stephen Dawson. Their idea was that *'you could take the formula used to grow a promising business and apply these to the best charities and social enterprises.'*

181

Today, led by Andy Ratcliffe (p188), Impetus-PEF is a leading giver of investment and expertise to Britain's most exciting charities working with disadvantaged young people. And we both sit on its Board.

Late to leadership

Nat took an unusual route to social sector leadership in two respects. First, he came to it relatively late, in his mid-40s. The first 25 years of his working life were spent forming, buying, selling and advising companies, both as an entrepreneur and for major corporates like Accenture.

Second, Nat challenged, straight-off, some of the dominant ideas about how the social sector could succeed. He's continued to do so since taking up his most prominent current role as Chair of Big Lottery Fund England.

BIG LOTTERY FUND ENGLAND
- Big Lottery Fund is a non-departmental public body responsible for distributing funds raised by the National Lottery for good causes
- Since 2004 it has awarded over £6 billion to more than 130,000 projects in the UK
- As Chair of the Big Lottery Fund since 2011, Nat Sloane has helped move £700m of BL investment towards longer term funding for local organisations doing pioneering things in close partnership with local government and business.

Strong family influence

Like many social leaders, Nat has been influenced by his close family – initially his parents and later his wife.

As a young child, Nat would accompany his entrepreneur father around the factories of Cleveland, (*'the Sheffield of the Mid-West'*) on Saturday mornings, taking it all in. Then in the afternoon, his Dad would volunteer with deprived, mainly black, youths in downtown Cleveland. Something about doing well and doing good was sown at that time.

But it didn't manifest until much later, well into his marriage when Nat noticed the impact his wife was having as a reading tutor in a school:

'I would come home after a day helping a team of execs at a multinational make more money and we would talk about what we'd been doing. She was teaching kids from disadvantaged areas to build life skills, maths, reading, how to work together. I realised then I had to do more with my life.'

Urgency around this was added by the fact that Nat's own father had died relatively young. *'I knew I shouldn't hang around,'* he says.

So he got involved in a few Boards, met a few trusts and foundations and came to the conclusion that there was nobody working with social purpose organisations in the way that he worked with his own clients: by investing long-term, by injecting expertise in key areas of the organisation to accelerate growth.

'I was looking for social entrepreneurs with performance anxiety and a thirst for innovation and particularly those willing to work closely with an investor.'

The Impetus effect

Hence, Impetus – and our first meeting fifteen years ago. About a year after that, my own organisation, VoiceAbility, received £400k from Impetus in cash and the equivalent, over several years, of in-kind support.

From there, I turned a promising-but-shambolic £500k local charity working with very small numbers into a professionally-run national organisation that today turns over nearly £10m and touches thousands of lives each year.

Today, Nat reflects on the learning from Impetus and makes three points. First, *'it was much harder than we thought it was going to be to find the social entrepreneurs who were up for this. It's a more complicated conversation than it is with a growing business.'*

Next, he came to understand more about the importance to success of alignment between Impetus and senior teams and boards in the social sector. All of which, he says, need to embrace a very hands-on type of funder.

'At first, we backed the leader as much as the venture and took the view that all would be fine if a Board did no harm. I realised we had to work as purposefully with the Boards as the CEOs.'

Lastly, Nat learned that, to have the widest possible impact, social sector organisations needed to find a way of working with the state. *'For many years, I would rather stick needles in my eyes than work with government, but I realised that, whatever the cultural friction and pain, the result is often worth it.'*

Leading at the Lottery

Nat's next big role in 2011 was as Chair of the Big Lottery

Fund in England. Six years on, he sees social change arising from the impact created by initiatives that start in communities and go from there.

Under Nat's leadership in England, the Big Lottery Fund has backed a range of initiatives like Power to Change (an independently endowed trust to catalyse community businesses) and strategic programmes like Talent Match (getting young people far from the job market into work) and Ageing Better (community initiatives led by older people to reduce social isolation).

All are designed to go on to influence policy and wider practice. While acknowledging the role of the larger charities, Nat is strongly of the view that *'the smaller end of the social sector is often where the really interesting work is going on.'*

On social investment
The third part of Nat's portfolio as a social sector leader is as founding chair of Social and Sustainable Capital (led by Ben Rick p195). Now one of the largest social finance intermediaries, it has raised £50m.

Nat was an early evangelist of social investment as a way of bringing more money into the sector. Today, he is less convinced that this market will achieve the scale he originally anticipated: *'Social investment is still a cottage industry and may always be – this is a very hard market for charities and for those seeking to offer finance.'*

Learnings for leaders
What can we learn from Nat as a social leader? While his use of private sector methods has become more

nuanced, his insight that we need to provide highly engaged, commercially-minded backing to high-potential organisations is important. Few people were saying this 20 years ago. Today, it is accepted by most trusts and foundations, many of whom now operate in a similar way.

Nat's first piece of advice for tomorrow's social sector leaders will be familiar: '*You have to be bloody resilient! There is no financial upside in the social sector – there has to be long-term motivation beyond the self.*' His second is to develop a good team. '*The best leaders I have encountered are people who know how to build a team around them, different skills, perspectives; who don't mind a challenge.*'

And the third is from Woody Allen: '*I think a big part of success is, 'showing up' – get stuck in, stay stuck in. Social change is a long-term challenge; you have to be prepared to stick with it for a while.*'

Nat turned 64 in 2017, an age when many choose to retire. 2015 saw him at Buckingham Palace to receive a CBE for services to venture philanthropy so he could easily sit back and rest on his laurels. But retirement is the last thing on his mind. Nat also has business interests in the USA and, in the UK, a range of philanthropic board memberships: '*I make my money in the USA, I spend it here in the UK,*' he smiles.

I end where I started, with Nat's own influence on me as a social leader. He spotted potential in me that many couldn't, including, at times, myself. He saw beyond my nervous stammer and shoes from Matalan. He then backed me with his own hard-won cash – and made me want to do it for him as much as anyone else. That is true social leadership.

Key Points from Nat:

1. Venture-philanthropy is about investing big and long-term behind the most promising social entrepreneurs, ideas and organisations.
2. Finding organisations that respond well to this approach isn't as easy in the social sector as it is in business.
3. Social sector success normally means working with the state, however culturally dissonant this might be.
4. Community-led, cross sector collaboration is vital to social sector success – so make the effort to build partnerships that can really add value and impact to what you're there to do.
5. Social investment is not turning out how many thought it might, growth being much slower than anticipated.

Andy Ratcliffe, CEO, Impetus-PEF
www.impetus-pef.org.uk @andyratcliffe9

'Social investors, as well as venture philanthropists are our stakeholders and their success is important to us. But the ultimate test for us is, does it deliver better results for young people?'

The playing field

It was going to a struggling West Midlands secondary school that first kindled Andy Ratcliffe's interest in the inequalities in our education system. Many of his classmates were failed by the system – missing out on the GCSEs they needed to stay in education. With the help of his mum and some competition from his 'much cleverer' best friend, Andy did well at school and went on to study PPE at Oxford University.

'A lot of my mates at school would have had different options and experience, had they been in a different school or part of the country,' Andy explains. This was something he knew that one day he would try to do something about.

Measures of poverty

At Oxford, Andy's social network changed. Here, he was mixing with people who grew up in wealthy families and had been to good private schools. It felt wrong to him that parental wealth could dictate your future success.

He followed his degree with an MSc in comparative social policy and set out on a career as a researcher. His early work involved developing measures of UK poverty that could inform policy. Some of the work he did then is still used today.

He also researched poverty in South Africa, a country with a yawning gap between the privileged elites and the far poorer black population. Apartheid might have been abolished ten years earlier, but, in 2003, your life chances still depended on the colour of your skin.

Goodbye academia

Over time, academia lost its appeal to Andy. It was OK to research and study poverty, quite another to do something about it.

So, Andy joined the UK civil service, ultimately becoming a senior policy adviser on education in the Prime Minister's Strategy Unit. This gave him opportunity to shape policy, or so he thought. In reality, Prime Minister Gordon Brown was not expected to remain in power long, meaning there was little appetite for radical change.

Andy moved on to a new role where he felt he could have impact. He joined the Tony Blair Africa Governance Initiative (AGI) and moved to Rwanda.

The fact is, he tells me, that effective government is as key to delivering social change in African nations as it is the UK. Too often, the machinery to deliver what a newly elected government wants to see simply does not exist. AGI exists to help develop the systems and processes that can deliver that change.

Onto African realities
Andy describes Rwanda as *'an optimistic and uplifting place to live and work.'*

Although our minds are always drawn to the Rwandan genocide in 1994 through the early years of this century, Rwanda was one of the ten fastest growing economies in the world. Fertile land, a gentle equatorial climate and an enterprising people made it, for Andy, a great place to live and work.

Into charity
Then one day a head-hunter called. It was, said Andy, one of those *'do you know anyone who might be interested,'* calls. He took the call as he genuinely wanted to help. But when the role of CEO at Impetus was described to him, he felt compelled to find out more.

IMPETUS-PEF

- Impetus is a Private Equity Foundation (Impetus-PEF) transforming the lives of economically disadvantaged 11–24-year-olds, by ensuring they get the support they need to succeed in education, find and keep jobs, and achieve their potential
- Funded by the private equity industry itself, Impetus makes philanthropic investments in charities that can level the playing field in education and jobs
- Becoming CEO in 2016, Andy Ratcliffe has furthered the Impetus quest to find, fund and build the most promising charities working towards that mission.

The focus of Impetus is education; it was right up Andy's street.

'When I applied for the job, I showed them my school class photo, because a lot of people on it were smart, but didn't get the same chances, or they were expelled,' he says. His mother was a careers adviser, so he grew up understanding the employability problems that followed a poor education.

A partner, not just a funder

Soon, Andy was CEO of Impetus-PEF. While traditional grant-makers welcome unsolicited applications, then select grant recipients and check to see the impact a grant has made, Impetus goes much further. Its people, Andy tells me, get to really know the charities they choose to support and work alongside them to ensure their programmes can really change lives.

The Impetus team then works shoulder-to-shoulder with the leadership of each charity, spending as much as a day a week with each organisation.

Funding is, of course, only part of growing a successful charity. Often, help is needed with programme design, governance, financial management and much more. Impetus works as partners first, funders second.

Impetus, Andy underlines, can offer an enviable network of professionals willing to provide pro bono expertise that otherwise simply would not be affordable by the growing charity. It also distributes a far from modest £4m a year in grants, so can have significant influence.

When you're ready for social investment
For Impetus, social investment is only one way to help charities reach more young people. Grant funding can only take you so far, Andy says, *'but you need scale and momentum to be able to repay social investment.'*

Again, unlike most grant makers, when a charity in the portfolio is ready for social investment, Andy's team introduces suitable investors. *'We support both the charity and the investor to make sure the deal they do works for both parties,'* explains Andy.

Once working with Impetus, a charity can expect support over a number of years. Again, this sets them apart from many other players in the charity funding world. Sustainability is important to Andy and his team.

The government is particularly risk-averse
From national government to local councils, there is reluctance, Andy observes, to commission anything that carries any perceived risk. This can create inertia; with the view sometimes held that it's better to do nothing, than risk

something going wrong. Andy, and many of the Impetus portfolio charities, has had to deal with this, even in the face of strong evidence of impact.

Andy's view today is that big change can come about as a consequence of many small changes. He believes that real change will come from the grassroots, rather than the top.

Becoming a CEO for the first time really makes you think
While Andy had a big job at AGI, Impetus is his first CEO role.

'When I walked in the first time to meet the team, I had a big gulp moment,' he admits, *'even though, with 35 people, the team is quite small.'* With a relaxed leadership style, Andy tends to win support. *'I think everyone knows that I am personally committed to making a difference.'*

Born curious
Andy claims that, as well as caring about the mission of the organisation, he is also innately curious. It was curiosity that probably helped him succeed at an indifferent school and go on to Oxford. That same curiosity leads him to ask his team lots of questions. *'They've had to learn that I ask questions – not to challenge or instruct, but because I genuinely want to understand.'*

Describing himself as an insatiable reader, Andy consumes both fiction and non-fiction at a fair pace, worrying if he's not got a pile of books ready to read. His wife tolerates his rapidly growing book collection and challenges him to leave a little space in their home for other things.

Family is important to Andy. He's spent time living on a different continent to his wife and so values their time together more as a result. He also regularly meets up with what he calls his 'core four' – a small group of friends he's had since university. He believes that maintaining good friendships can help keep your life in perspective. He's also a keen cyclist and reckons he does his best thinking when out on his bike.

Key Points from Andy:
1. Research can tell you a lot about social problems, but new policy and action are required to bring about change.
2. Grants can help you grow your organisation and its impact. But, unless your systems and processes evolve too, that growth might not be sustainable.
3. If you're working in a disadvantaged community, you can only influence so much. This can and will go off track, often for reasons you could never influence.
4. Reading widely, including fiction, can broaden your perspective on life and your work. Sometimes, you get the best ideas from the least likely book.
5. The deep understanding of the lives of others you only gain from close friends can help you keep your life in perspective.

Ben Rick, Managing Partner, SASC
www.socialandsustainable.com
@SASCapital

'It's been tough building a business in such a new and unforgiving marketplace.'

The money measure
The bonuses earned by City traders have always been controversial. It's a frenetic world dominated by bright young men. They learn quickly to accept that not every deal pays off, moving quickly on to the next opportunity. More often, they generate significant profits for their employers, which is how they come to earn those large bonuses. It's a world where everything is measured in monetary terms.

At first glance, investment banking and social enterprise are poles apart. Yet, Ben Rick walked away from a successful life in investment banking to work in a sector he feels passionate about. *'After a while,* he says, *'you start to hate the life you lead and yearn for a life where you can make a difference, not just cash.'*

195

Before entering the social investment market, Ben had years of commercial investment experience. He says we'd be kidding ourselves if we believed that large corporates were always more professional or effective than charities or social enterprises. He was trading throughout the 2008 crisis and undoubtedly could tell some tales.

Good prep

A degree in management science, together with an ability to think quickly, led Ben to a successful City career. He ended up as European Head of Global Proprietary Trading at Bank of America Merrill Lynch, but gave it all up in 2011, after six months at a hedge fund. By then married with a young family, he wanted to see his children grow up and find a purpose beyond profit.

Ben had already become philanthropic, supporting charities with which he found resonance. He thought about a change of career, but realised that his skills did not equip him well for an operational role with a charity. He left his City job and took time to reflect and plan his next move.

Band of escapees

It was in early 2012 that Ben met another City escapee, Adam Knight, who was in a similar situation. Adam had a contact at Big Issue Invest, which led to a conversation with Sir Ronald Cohen and then the newly formed Big Society Capital.

The social investment market was slowly emerging and Big Society Capital was keen to see new intermediaries enter the market. Ben and Adam had no direct experience of third sector financing but did understand investment. In September 2012, they established Social and Sustainable Capital (SASC) as a new social impact investor.

SOCIAL AND SUSTAINABLE CAPITAL (SASC)
- SASC provides simple finance for extraordinary charities and social enterprises – flexible capital to enable social sector organisations to grow their social impact, improving the lives of disadvantaged people across the UK
- The company enables greater access to the right kind of investment which makes charities and social enterprises better able to tackle society's most pressing challenges
- Joint-founder of SASC, Ben Rick, launched the business in 2013 and, in 2017, saw it produce its first impact report.

Bumpy beginnings

With government austerity starting to bite, Ben and Adam could see that the market for social enterprises was changing, with a new generation of social entrepreneurs emerging from the public sector. Here were people with a different approach to finance than those running charities, for whom grant funding and public commissioning had been the norm.

Of course, it is never easy to enter a new market and SASC had a bumpy ride as it strove to make its mark. The start-up phase lasted longer than hoped, but, almost five years in, Ben feels like SASC is hitting its stride.

Social investment is all about relationships

The SASC approach is all about relationships. With a team of just nine, those seeking investment often get to meet many of the team during the application process.

In some situations, SASC is able to blend loans with grant funding. Social investment alone is not always the answer with grant funding needed to ensure a step change to a sustainable business model.

SASC also manages money for The Social Investment Business and has partnered with Santander on its Third Sector Investment Fund.

Not every case presented wins support. For some, the simple economic facts defeat them. Investment without the revenue to repay it simply builds an organisation up for an even harder fall than it is already facing.

Social investment has been slower to take off than hoped
SASC's marketplace is all about risk. The reluctance of high street banks to lend to small business is well documented. Investing in not-for-profit organisations for anything other than bricks and mortar lending is almost always a step too far.

But there's also risk aversion from charities to borrow. Just because social investors are prepared to finance organisations to grow doesn't mean they always want to take it.

'We have had to adapt quickly to respond to some of the unexpected headwinds we have experienced, but are now seeing steady growth in the number of investible deals coming forward.'

Ben also believes that the social sector should pay what it needs to attract the right skills. He hopes that social investment will get to the point where it can be a sound career choice for someone fresh from university. Too often, people change from a commercial role in mid-life, when income becomes less of a driver. Ben perhaps illustrates that point well, founding SASC when he turned 40.

It's about the impact, but we must always consider the risk
In social investment, there are additional non-financial considerations that you have to be very sure about before you go on the investment journey with a social enterprise.

Saying no to an enthusiastic social entrepreneur seeking funding can be difficult. This is especially true when you feel an emotional connection with the project in which you're asked to invest. *'I'll not say which of our portfolio of investments give me the greatest sense of satisfaction,'* explains Ben. *'We need to remain professional and objective, even if it hurts inside when you have to say no.'*

It can be too easy, Ben feels, to kid yourself that a failing social enterprise can be saved by social investment. If an enterprise in which SASC has invested starts to falter, much work goes into trying to help turn the situation round. But, Ben is clear that throwing more money into a struggling enterprise may only delay the inevitable. His trading days taught him that you have to cut your losses and move on. That, he says, is as true today as it's always been.

Ben's motivation for starting his business was to play a small part in making our world a better place. He also wanted to have time to watch his children grow up – not be one of those fathers who simply pops his head round the door at bedtime to say goodnight.

199

He manages his diary so that he can walk his children to school each day. In fact, it was at the school gate that he got to know Adam Knight, SASC's co-founder.

Surprisingly perhaps, for someone living in London, Ben has taken to horse-riding. It started when he took his children for lessons, but soon he was also in the saddle. It is, he says, one of the few places where he is forced to concentrate on the task in hand and forget about work for a while.

His eldest is about to start secondary school. So, being walked to school by dad might lose its appeal. Ben chose the right moment to move from the City to something more balanced in every way. Many of us can learn from that.

Key Points from Ben:
1. **Social investors are as interested in the team as the business proposition. Good teams – level-headed yet compassionate – are what an investor wants to see.**
2. **The risk/reward balance in social investment is a work in progress, and may take some time to develop into a fully functional marketplace.**
3. **Don't assume big business is any better than small social enterprise. You get good and bad operations in all sectors.**
4. **Innovation driven by a determination to improve the lives of others can be powerful. What remains to be seen is how often it can be scalable.**
5. **However hard you work, remember that making time for family is the most important thing of all.**

SECTION NINE:

FUTURE LEADERSHIP

'People learn that the private sector are not all super-efficient demi-gods and that the third sector are not all angels with halos. Many are caught up in survival rather than thinking about how they can dramatically grow their impact through deep and powerful partnerships. So we take them to Tesla, where the ambition is to go to Mars.'

Liam Black, Chief Encouragement Officer, Wavelength

Introduction

What will it take for social leaders to change the
world as we move towards the 2020s? What will
be different? How might we need to adapt?

Three big domestic worries loom over the future
of the UK. The first is demographics. Britain is
a rapidly ageing country with nearly 12 million
people over 65 and 1.5m over the age of 85. The second is
the UK economy, which is failing young people, many of
whom are now far or less well-off than their parents were by
the age of 30. The third is inequality, particularly in health
and education.

People in the poorer north now live markedly shorter lives
than those in the more prosperous south. Kids born to
the poorest parents are more likely than ever to be poor
or unskilled as adults. Compounding all of this is a more
complex, fragmented society in which social solutions have
to become increasingly sophisticated.

The social sector environment isn't going to be easy, either.
Government has struggled to engage effectively with all of
these problems. This hasn't always been for want of trying.

*challenge
scale*

It is widely understood that solutions to complex problems are less likely to come 'top-down' from big institutions but, instead, from the bottom-up. From organisations like ours. From leaders like us and the people who succeed us. This book abounds with such examples, from Paul Sinton-Hewitt's parkrun (pp 32-38), which is about health and community, to Brett Wigdortz's Teach First, a social business, now the biggest employer of young graduates (pp 39-45) in Britain.

In this final section, we explore the views of three people who are looking at the future through different lenses.

Karl Wilding heads Public Policy and Volunteering at the National Council for Voluntary Organisations. He sees in particular the importance of the decline of the state and the rise of the 'millennial' generation in future social change. Finding new ways to harness their social concern is a key challenge, he says. This includes a faster move to digital and a greater diversity of people and perspectives in our sector.

Andy Hillier looks at the social sector through the lens of the media. He edits *Third Sector*, the charity sector's trade magazine, and sees a sector badly neglected by government that needs to make its own future for itself and reassert its independence.

Finally, **Professor Andy Wood** examines the sector as both a corporate CEO and an academic. In his day job, Andy runs Adnams plc, a highly progressive corporate that measures its success by more than its profit. His view is that social sector leaders need to embrace business more as potential partners, rather than seeing business as part of the problem.

Karl Wilding,
Director of Policy and Volunteering, NCVO
www.ncvo.org.uk @karlwilding

'Social change is hard, it is not linear, it zig-zags, you make progress, then someone will tell you you're wrong. Stick at it!'

Never linear

Karl Wilding was born and bred a few miles from me in rainy, post-industrial Blackburn, Lancashire. From witnessing the town's decline in the '80s and '90s, Karl is more aware than most that progress isn't a one-way street: *'Achieving social change is never linear,'* he says, *'you can zig-zag – and go backwards.'*

Like me, Karl left the north-west of England at 18 to attend a redbrick university to study in the social sciences. He flirted briefly with becoming a teacher, did a PhD instead and then got a research job with the National Council for Voluntary Organisations (NCVO), *'a body that represents and helps a sector I love.'* Where, almost 20 years on, he is now Director for Policy and Volunteering.

Decline of the state
Karl is in the book because he has a uniquely sharp eye for trends. For many years, he's been the force behind the *Civil Society Almanac,* a big book published annually by NCVO, full of hard research on our sector. But Karl also has powerful instincts on what's coming down the track and what this means for people leading social change.

So, what does Karl see in the future for our sector? He cites three really important developments.

The first is the big new gap in support for our most vulnerable people created by the retreat of both the state and the family over the last 30 years. *'This ramps up demand on community-level organisations,'* he tells me. *'Our sector becomes, in effect, a substitute family to many people.'*

Our primary job as social leaders in this situation, *'isn't necessarily to lobby for more public services (though there may be a place for that), but to come up with ever more sophisticated means for people to help each other.'* To create a new kind of social fabric.

We talk about parkrun (see p32) as a really powerful contemporary example of how communities can be brought together, informally, to have their overall needs met. In the case of parkrun, it might be the volunteer marshal coping with bereavement or the 50-year-old runner getting his blood pressure down on doctor's orders. *'I love parkrun,'* says Karl, *'it is the shape of things to come – not a 'service' as such, in the conventionally understood way, but doing a service.'*

Rise of the millennials

The second trend Karl thinks is significant is that of 'millennials' – those born between 1982 and 2000. *'I think we have a millennial generation more socially conscious than any generation since before the Second World War.'* The social leadership challenge, says Karl, is that *'we have to find better ways to harness the millennials than we do now.'*

'Much of the social sector,' he says, *'is based on the Baby-Boomers and the idea that people still segment their lives into 'work' and that which they do 'for good' later in the form of philanthropy or volunteering.'* This business model of the social sector, Karl argues, doesn't suit the millennial generation who don't want to leave 'doing good' till later or outsource it all to charities. Instead, they want to make an impact now and they want to do it where they are, whether that is private banking or public administration. Millennials are, he says, 'sector-blind'.

To enable and support this generation, future social sector leaders have, Karl says, *'to transform their organisations away from being fundraising and delivery machines to becoming enablers of those who want to find their own ways of making a difference.'* It's a new business-model and one that very few charities have yet to embrace.

The future is digital

The third trend all social leaders need to understand better, Karl argues, is digitalisation: *'People's lived experience is now digital in many walks of their lives, even when dealing with parts of the state. And this is moving faster than many social sector organisations' own business models,'* he says.

We have only seen the beginning of this. One area where digital is making fast headway, and shining a light on the future, is 'GiveDirectly.org'. This an American charity now opening in London that allows donors to directly fund an individual with no 'middleman' charity taking up to half of that money in costs. *'Such disintermediation,'* Karl says, *'is clearly an existential threat to social sector organisations unable or unwilling to be able to give a similar, real-time picture of outcome.'*

Breaking bad habits

All three of these trends, Karl says, are addressable. But to do so, the sector needs to consciously move out of some of its long-standing ways. The social sector, especially to the generation coming through, can seem *'clunking and slow,'* he says. Getting anything done in many of our organisations involves *'cutting through layers of sedimentary rock, so intricate are many of our systems and processes.'*

'There is a usefulness to our sector's rigour,' he says, *'not least at times, not least when public confidence in charities is low.'* It remains the case, Karl says, *'that successful social sector organisations will, in the future, have to become far quicker at both starting new things – and stopping old ones.'*

Driving for diversity

While Karl believes the social sector has to become better at developing our own leaders, he makes a powerful and original point about diversity, which I will quote in full.

'There is a group think in our sector. When I speak in public I ask for a show of hands on the EU Referendum and nearly all people voted Remain. Yet, in many of the poorest places in Britain, Brexit was the best day of many people's lives.'

What Karl is pointing to here is that successful social leadership means we have to be really open in our thinking: to accept that those outside our politics also want to make a difference, and will have their own ideas of the 'good'.

Key Points from Karl:
1. **The institutions that sustained society in the 20th century – the state and the family – are both in retreat, leaving social sector organisations with bigger demand in the 21st century.**
2. **The millennial generation want to make an impact now not later and from whichever sector they are in – and social leaders need to gear up their organisations to enable this.**
3. **Digitalisation is changing everything faster than most social leaders understand – and moving towards this from what we have now is one of our single biggest leadership challenges.**
4. **Diversity in the sector isn't just about gender, race and sexuality, it is also about including people from a wider range of political perspectives and accepting their validity.**
5. **Social change is long-term, not linear and requires social leaders to pace themselves accordingly.**

Andy Hillier, Editor, Third Sector
www.thirdsector.co.uk @andy_hillier

'Third sector organisations will continue to be needed and won't be displaced any time soon.'

Early inspiration
Andy Hillier decided to become a journalist when he was 14 years old. He fulfilled this ambition quickly, in 1998, just at the time when the internet was transforming news formats. He rose gradually through the ranks to become Editor of *Third Sector*, the main trade publication and news website for the social sector in 2016.

We meet at Haymarket's vast base in Twickenham, London, where teams of journalists across four floors work on titles as diverse as *FourFourTwo* – a football monthly – to *Management Today*.

A sector silenced?

Andy has three specific concerns about the state of our sector as we approach the 2020s. The first is about the way the social sector leaders have been treated by government:

'There is a lot of justified unease and upset about the way the charity sector has been treated through cuts to its finances through central government. Social sector leaders have become cautious about what they say publicly at times, especially those reliant on local or national government funding.'

Pet projects

Andy's second concern is the way that Office for Civil Society funding has been funnelled into a small number of government 'pet' projects, with little regard of the wider needs of the sector. He says: *'For example, we have seen the radical scaling up of the National Citizen Service, but does it warrant taking the lion's share of the OCS's funding – £1.25bn over this Parliament – especially given the funding difficulties faced by charity sector?'*

In a similar way, Andy feels that the way that more than £500m of Libor fines money - collected from City institutions following the rigging of the inter-bank lending rate - has been distributed, largely to armed forces and emergency services charities, comes across as a *'political decision'*.

'What is unique about these charities that places them above the rest of the sector? It feels like a political decision: one that plays well with older Conservative voters and in the Home Counties but it just doesn't feel quite right and fair. The money raised from the fines could have made a significant difference across a broader range of charities.'

Social investment hype

Third is Andy's worry about social investment, which has attracted considerable government time and money: *'I think we are entering a new phase where we are seeing a recognition that this has been overhyped, and is not the silver bullet that the government appeared to be promising.'* The fact that social finance isn't really working as expected is a real worry: *'We have seen some interesting organisations benefit from the funding, but the investment seems to follow the trend of investing in new and innovative projects, rather than helping established social sector organisations to get better.'*

Is bigger better?

He also wonders what will be the long-term implications of offering ever bigger contracts. He asks: *'Do they deliver better results? Are they cheaper long term? And what happens to smaller organisations' beneficiaries if they lose contracts? I don't believe that small is good and big is bad, but we have to ask what happens long term when contracts are awarded to big players.'* Andy suggests that a better approach might be for large and small social sector organisations to work together.

Big talent pool

Does Andy see any cause for optimism? Thankfully, he does. The sector's emerging cohort of CEOs and senior leaders including Matt Hyde (p113), Simon Blake (p96) and Julie Bentley (p13) is, he thinks, of exceptional quality *'just as good if not better than in any other sector'* despite a chronic lack of investment in leadership development. He also believes that Theresa May's government is more sympathetic to the sector than that of her predecessor, David Cameron.

Commercial titans?

Andy believes that more social sector organisations could end up following the lead of charities such as Nuffield Health, St Andrew's Healthcare and the Consumers' Association and operate more like commercial business than traditional charities.

A more caring society

Andy does see promise in the future. The political environment in the UK has changed over the past year. The public made it clear in the general election of 2017 that it wants a more equal and caring society. Andy says that the third sector needs to hold the government to account on its commitment to create a 'shared society' and support people who are struggling.

Key Points from Andy:

1. **Government has not treated the social sector particularly well during the past decade and has stifled its independent voice.**
2. **Central government funding that should have been spent on addressing a range of social problems has been diverted in too many cases to the government's favoured projects, with little involvement of the sector itself.**
3. **Social investment plays a helpful role in social sector finance but has delivered far less than was anticipated.**
4. **Leadership in the social sector is of exceptional quality despite a serious lack of investment.**
5. **The growth in the size of government contracts has led to a smaller number of highly commercialised charities being in a position to compete, leaving smaller and medium-sized charities in a difficult space.**

Professor Andy Wood, CEO, Adnams plc
www.adnams.co.uk @AndyatAdnams

'*I don't subscribe to the idea of a leader as someone on a white charger, sword drawn. In a modern, complex organisation, it takes more than one person to lead, indeed there are times when colleagues take on massive leadership roles.*'

Don't moralise!

We meet at the HQ of Adnams plc, a £70m turnover business, in the quaint Suffolk coastal town of Southwold. Adnams' brewery sits, as it has since 1872, bang in the centre of town. Its CEO, Andy Wood has successfully led the company for the better part of 20 years.

But, like many corporate leaders, his concern for business is equalled by his concern for our society and our planet. Indeed, like Paul Polman, CEO of Unilever, another socially responsible business, he does not see them as necessarily separate.

I kick off with a direct question: 'Can charities and social enterprises learn from the most progressive private companies?'

'*Yes, they can*' is the view of Andy who is one of a growing band of socially-oriented private sector CEOs who believes that charities and social enterprises do not have a monopoly on social good.

'*I sometimes see an inverted snobbery – the for-profit sector seen as rapacious; stabbing each other in the back while the third sector – we do good work. I think this is a mistaken view.*'

He points out that all organisations, whether private or charitable, tend in reality to produce a mixture of outcomes. It makes more sense, he thinks, to look at what an organisation actually does, not at its legal status.

The Adnams way
Andy likes to walk his talk. In recent years, he tells me, Adnams invested more than was technically necessary, in a state-of-art eco-storage facility in Southwold – where grass grows on the roof of where they keep the beer.

The 550 staff at Adnams are, Andy says, treated well. Redundancies are largely avoided, even in bad times. This is because staff need to trust that the company truly cares. This care extends outside the business; Adnams invests a percentage of profit (via its own charitable trust) into largely small organisations within 25 miles of Southwold.

Passion for social mobility
So what fires Andy up? Social mobility is a passion. Andy likes to break glass ceilings wherever he sees them.

To make the point, he tells me the story of his Chief Operating Officer, Karen Hester. Karen started out in Adnams as a cleaner 25 years ago. Now she runs all of the company's operations as COO. *'It is one of the things of which I am most proud that we spotted Karen's talent and that she is doing brilliantly as COO today. It sends a powerful message.'*

On the Chair-CEO dynamic
One straight read-across sectors is the successful relationship between Andy and his Chair, Jonathan Adnams (whose family own part of the business).

'We share the same vision of where we want to take the company.' This relationship Andy describes as *'an ongoing conversation, pretty informal to be honest, characterised by a deep trust and mutual regard.'*

The relationship is, challenging, as it is supposed to be, but viewed by each as a value-creation partnership, more than the sum of its parts. *'It's important,'* Andy says, *'for CEO and Chair to be in constant dialogue, not just the set-piece governance meetings.'*

On building a culture
Another very obvious area of cross-sector learning concerns people, culture and values. All managers at Adnams, including the CEO, are evaluated on how well they listen and communicate with others.

Andy is firm on the collective, distributed nature of leadership in the company, dismissing the 'white knight' view of the CEO. He is careful throughout not to talk about his achievements or ambitions, only those of the company as a whole. There is no room, in his world, for large egos.

Coping with competition
Is it fair to draw lessons from the world of successful commercial brewing, retail and leisure then apply them within the UK voluntary sector in the 2020s?

Absolutely, in Andy's view: *'Adnams, in all its sectors, has, like many charities, had to cope with massive, very rapid changes in its world: the rise of craft brewing, the precipitous decline of the pub trade and the fact that people are drinking a lot less alcohol.'*

As part of a successful team, Andy worked with others to drive the successful expansion of Adnams from just brewing beer into wines, spirits, hotels and shops.

All this has meant that the company has had to develop one key capability above all others: that of adaptability. This one trait is, Andy believes, the key to Adnams success in weathering various storms. And the key attribute he tries to develop in all of his managers and staff.

Mid-sized doesn't mean 'caught in the middle'
Andy has some helpful thoughts on strategy for mid-sized social sector organisations. Adnams is neither a micro-brewery nor a big brand.

Indeed, it has made a virtue of its size. Adnams is more agile than the big players in terms of speed of response but more capable than the smaller players in capitalising on trends.

Beleaguered middle-order UK charities take heed!

On the need for commercial DNA

Andy thinks there are future commercial lessons from well-run companies like Adnams that any charity CEO could use.

'We have long time-horizon. There is patient capital in the organisation that is investing for the long-term success of the business on all fronts. There is a small but growing proportion of the business that is employee-owned. There is a way of working with people that isn't paternalistic but takes an interest in people in the right ways.'

On being a CEO

Like many CEOs, Andy views the role as intrinsically lonely: *'I remember the British boxer Antony Joshua's remark that he had 15 people walking with him from the dressing room to the ring but once the bell rings he is on his own.'*

Andy mitigates this, he says, by building a strong set of senior relationships, a tight team where senior people talk properly to each other and have a lot of informal conversations.

Andy is very clear on the importance of culture now and in the future – and the leader's role in holding it. *'Culture,'* he says, *'is like an atmosphere. We have at Adnams a strong sense of pride and loyalty in the business. It can therefore be difficult, at times, for outsiders, if they hit that atmosphere at the wrong trajectory. But the culture is what gives this business a key advantage so we protect and nurture it.'*

How can social sector leaders get their message 'out there'? Andy is clear on this: *'There is a "formal organisation" but there is also an informal network of how things really get done in an organisation. As the boss, you need to know how both the informal and formal organisation works.'*

Equally important for Andy is the authenticity of the message: *'It is easy to either clothe difficult messages in corporate PR-speak or, worse, to use governance niceties to avoid saying much at all of any interest. To be a great CEO,'* he says, *'you must be prepared to speak out.'*

Personal and professional growth

How does Andy survive, thrive and grow as a Chief Executive? He points to three main areas. Firstly, he keeps extremely fit and healthy. He eats mainly plant-based food and runs the odd marathon. Despite being in his late 50s, Andy could comfortably pass as a 40-year-old. He meditates daily, *'I use mindfulness and meditation to stay mentally fit and headspace in this job is vitally important.'*

Like most of our CEOs, Andy loves to read. At time of writing he was reading *The Book of Joy* by the Dalai Lama and Desmond Tutu.

How would Andy like to be remembered? *'Having played a part in an organisation that will endure another 140 years. It will also be important to be remembered as having been a good friend to people.'*

Key Points from Andy:
1. **Charities and social businesses can learn from progressive private companies.**

2. What an organisation does is more important than its legal status.
3. The CEO/Chair relationship should be built on deep trust and mutual respect.
4. You should try to turn your culture into a strategic advantage in your sector.
5. As a CEO you must be prepared to speak out, even when the message is not an easy one to deliver.

SECTION TEN:

YOUR LEADERSHIP

'Rather than setting up a charity and raising money for mental health, why not set up a charity that mends bikes and employ people with mental health problems?'

Dan Corry, CEO, New Philanthropy Capital

And now it's over to you

This is where things get personal. You've read the book. Now it's time to work out what it means for you.

I started by telling you about my own leadership journey. My time as a frontline CEO ended early, probably because I couldn't see a way to achieve more – and I wasn't willing to sit back and collect a salary.

Since then, I have been fortunate to find a life helping others to lead. But, when I reflect, I could with some changes, have made a much bigger difference than I did.

In the same spirit, I invite you now to do the same.

If you've read this book, you're likely to be an aspiring or relatively new leader who is looking to make maximum impact; or a leader in the middle point of your journey thinking about making the second half count for more; or, like me, at some kind of ending, thinking about where to go next.

Think carefully about the following questions and fill in the boxes below:

Where am I succeeding and failing as a social sector leader?

How is the rest of my life looking with regards to relationships, health?

What is my 'End Game' in terms of the impact I want to make on the totality of the issue I care about most?

What are the main barriers to my achieving these things?

What are the three things I can do in the next year that will take me towards my leadership and personal goals?

Whoever you are, I hope this book has helped you to reflect and come up with some answers. Equally, the book may have raised as many questions for you as it has answered. Don't worry, this isn't unusual. It's what you do next that counts.

One of the things I have learned as this book has come together is that leaders do better when they are part of strong communities of peers, mentors and supporters. People to whom to turn for advice, insight or just a listening ear. Changing the world isn't easy. People fail as much as they succeed.

Finding a way to be a successful social sector leader, while also looking after yourself and those around you, is one of the hardest challenges there is. Which is why so many of us end up failing in at least one of these.

How to Change the World has, I hope, equipped you a little better to be a more effective leader of social change - but to do this while remaining a happy and healthy person. The two actually can go together, with the right habits and the right support around you.

Today, more than ever, there are opportunities for social sector leaders to develop themselves to their next level. Social Club is one of these. Many of the leaders in here are members. But there are many more.

It's time now for me to stop. And for you to begin.

Reading list

Many great ideas have been stimulated by reading a book. We hope that this book has helped you recognise opportunities too. The books listed below have all been found useful by the leaders who feature in this book. Some are business books and some novels with resonance with the reader's mission: You might find them useful too:

Sapiens: A Brief History of Humankind – Yuval Noah Harris, Vintage 2015

Infinite Jest – David Foster Wallace, Abacus 1997

Outliers: The Story of Success – Malcolm Gladwell, Penguin 2009

Leadership: Plain and Simple – Steve Radcliffe, Financial Times Press 2012

Boundaries – Henry Cloud, Zondervan 2002

Good to Great – Jim Collins, Random House 2001

The Conflict Resolution Handbook – Gary Furlong, Wiley 2006

Systems Thinking in the Public Sector – John Seddon, Triarchy 2008

Necessary Endings: The Employees, Businesses, and Relationships That All of Us Have to Give Up in Order to Move Forward – Henry Cloud, Harper Business 2011

Why Don't Students Like School? – Daniel Willingham, Jossey Bass 2010

Uncommon Service: How to Win by Putting Customers at the Core of Your Business – Francis Frei, Harvard Business Press 2012

How to Lead – Jo Owen, Pearson, 2015

About the author

Craig Dearden-Phillips is the author of three books on social sector leadership and is a Visiting Lecturer at London Cass Business School. He took his first charity CEO role at 25 and now coaches CEOs, boards and teams in the social sector to become more successful. Craig also runs Social Club, a fast-growing network of social sector leaders.

Beyond this, Craig is a Trustee of Impetus-PEF and is Chair of the Stepping Out Foundation which supports social start-ups. Outside work, Craig has three children, lives in Suffolk and is a committed amateur triathlete, representing Great Britain in 2017.